THE UNDERBURNER'S DIET

THE UNDERBURNER'S DIET

HOW TO KEEP YOUR BODY FROM STORING EXCESS FAT FOREVER

Barbara Edelstein, M.D., P.C.

MACMILLAN PUBLISHING COMPANY
NEW YORK

Macmillan Publishing Company
866 Third Avenue, New York, N.Y. 10022
Collier Macmillan Canada, Inc.

002-534940-6

Printed in the United States of America

For my patients—and their children

CONTENTS

ACKNOWLEDGMENTS

David Edelstein edited this book.
Jeffrey Edelstein added his two cents, sometimes more.
Carol Mull kept my office running while I scribbled.
Robert Stewart of Macmillan kept this book alive through
all the rewrites.
Richard Kaufman, M.D., did the medical reading.

INTRODUCTION: A CALORIE IS NOT ALWAYS A CALORIE

I have always suspected that there are differences in the way people gain and lose weight, differences more complicated than fat people eating more than thin people. As a child I didn't eat much and was chubby; my mother, meanwhile, gobbled chocolates all day and had a figure so terrific that my teachers used to dream up reasons to hold conferences.

The question must be asked: Is a calorie always a calorie? Is the blueberry muffin in one mouth the same as the blueberry muffin in another?

Common sense says that fat people eat more than thin people. A *lot* more. The term you hear most often is *overeaters,* which means that the heavyweights in question eat above and beyond what they need to stay alive. I used to buy that idea myself. But after three books and twenty-five years of practicing medicine, I am convinced that different bodies handle different foods differently. We have finally arrived at the real issue.

Consider Andi. Pretty and motivated. A paralegal. Five feet five inches and 160 pounds. Stalled. She'd lost weight and then gained it all back again, drifting up and down the scale like a yo-yo. Most of that time she ate like a fashion model—she nearly starved herself down to a "trim" 130.

"It's not that I eat everything I want," she told me the day she came back to the office, seething. "I haven't had an ice-cream cone in six months, and I have thin friends who eat them all the time.

"My life," she concluded, "has been one deprivation after another. I go on a diet that promises permanent weight loss. I lose some weight—terrific. New clothes, 'Gee you look great,' the whole bit. Then, before I know it, the new clothes are tight. It all creeps back, a little at a time, and it's not because I'm eating sundaes for lunch. I'm just eating like a normal person.

"I'm so sick of thinking about food every minute, and I'm sick of people who think I gorge myself when I go home at night. If those people put on weight the way I put on weight, they'd be a lot fatter than I am."

Looking at Andi, you have two choices. One is to believe her. But if you do, you'll have to make some radical adjustments in how you re-gard fat people. The other conclusion, more commonly reached, is that she's lying. The sorry truth is that she simply has no willpower or self-discipline—she's a "pig," a "glutton," a "cookie snitcher." If that's your point of view, you aren't alone. In 1963, Irving Pearlstein wrote an influential book called *Diet Is Not Enough*, in which he made the fol-lowing assertion: "The great majority of overweight persons gained the excess pounds not from deficient glands, but from deficient habits and attitudes, not from physical malady, but from psychological maladjust-ment."

That's been the prevailing attitude in the culture and the medical profession for a long, long time. And it wasn't my fat patients who made me suspect the idea was a crock. It was my thin ones. Hard as it is to believe, thin people actually come to me to help them gain weight. They're my favorites. "Drag yourself out of bed in the morning," I tell them. "Pry open that freezer and take out a quart of chocolate ice cream. Put three scoops in a blender, add some whole-fat milk and two —no, wait a minute, better make that three—tablespoons of chocolate syrup. Do you have any strawberries? Float 'em. Brush your teeth, take a shower, and let's get ready for a big breakfast . . ."

Do my patients gain weight? Some, a little. But the slightest bout of stress, sickness, or sleeplessness makes the pounds come tumbling off. They come back, their skinny arms hanging from their shirts, and weigh a mere half-pound more on a diet that would shoot my other patients up to three hundred pounds in less than a year. Watching these scrawny people struggle to add fat, I've seen more clearly than ever that *a calorie is not always a calorie.* A calorie in one mouth is less in a second, more in a third. It depends on the person's metabolism.

It's time for a new concept in the field of weight control to replace the dreaded "overeater." That concept is the *underburner.*

The underburner is, simply, someone whose body tends to store food as fat instead of converting it to heat and burning it off. Underburners are more, not less, energy-efficient than their thin counterparts. Their bodies run so well they get incredible mileage out of the least number of calories; they *conserve* energy. In a society as well-fed as ours, most people don't need a machine this efficient, but once, in primitive times, only those with the best storage systems stayed alive. When the climate is harsh and the food scarce, these people ensure the survival of the species. And it's no surprise that most underburners are female, since women are responsible for carrying both themselves and the next generation.

My poor, thin, overburning patients? There isn't much I can do for them. Certain blood pressure, birth control, and antidepressant medications make it easier to convert food to fat, but you don't want to start people on serious drugs unless their health is really threatened. In the end, all I can do is make sure they have enough vitamins and minerals to keep them going and counsel them to *enjoy* being skinny—to dress in layers, fluff up their hair, and smile. The icons of beauty in our society —the supermodels—are freakishly thin anyway, and so it isn't hard to make do with cheekbones too hollow, legs too willowy, or a waist too petite.

My underburners are another matter. In the last few years, I have devised a set of diets to help them drop the weight and keep it off, month after month: diets for *them* and not for genetic skinnies with a few rolls of post–New Year flab; diets for all phases of their lives, from adolescence to pregnancy to menopause. This book is the summation of these strategies.

Fad diets come and go. The books you'll want to keep are the ones that help you understand *why* you lose and gain, so you can control your weight even when you aren't dieting. My first effort, *The Woman Doctor's Diet for Women,* was written because I felt that females *didn't* understand how their bodies behaved when they tried to lose weight. They compared themselves to males, came out second best, and attributed their relative lack of success to a weakness in character. I tried to tell women they were different from men in the area of weight loss. Not better or worse, just different: in the number of calories they required to live, in the way they metabolized food, and in their hormones. Obviously, they needed to evaluate their diet and weight loss by *female* standards.

In the ten years since that book there has been new research in the field of weight control, and it points to one, inescapable conclusion: Some people, women and men, are born to be fatter and have a difficult time losing weight on almost all diets (even best-selling ones). So what do you do until science invents a pill to make all metabolisms equal? Continue to assume that everyone can lose the same amount of weight on any given diet? Or just give up and eat whatever you want?

Neither. You devise an entirely new strategy for losing weight and maintaining that weight loss. It isn't easy, but it's a lot easier when you aren't cutting calories in the dark.

If you're an underburner, this book will give you a variety of diets to lose weight steadily and to keep you from yo-yoing back a few months later. I'll tell you about every piece of food that goes into your mouth: which will fill you up, which will help your body burn calories, which will slow the process down, and which will help keep you from storming the cookie jar at midnight—when you're sure that only sugar, fat, and starch will make those cravings go away.

I'll also warn you about those times in your life when you have the greatest tendency to add new fat cells to your body—the most dangerous corners in an underburner's life. I'll explain how the first two decades can determine the shape of things to come and how you can choke off the tendency before you add those fatal pounds.

If you're not an underburner, this book can stop you from *becoming* one. There are periods in your life (pregnancy, menopause, the year you give up smoking) when metabolisms change dramatically, and people who've been able to shed five or ten pounds in a week or two of cutting out desserts suddenly find themselves spilling out of their clothes. My mother, in fact, finally has something to show for all those chocolates.

I want to give you knowledge of how your body works so that you can make responsible decisions about what goes or doesn't go into your mouth. Knowledge can keep you from despairing over the ease with which your body turns food into fat, and it can protect you from the glut of diet *mis*information in the culture—from the diet hucksters, the nutrition gurus, and the less-than-sympathetic psychologists.

Someday someone will invent a pill to change metabolisms, to make "normalweights" out of the most efficient underburners. Then we'll all slip into smashing outfits, I'll close my practice, and you can throw away your collection of useless diet books. In the meantime, let's learn how to burn.

Chapter 1

BORN TO BE FAT?

The Childhood and Adolescence of an Underburner

Let's review the statistics. If one of your parents is overweight, there's a 40 percent chance that you will be, too. If both parents are overweight, your chances jump to 80 percent. If neither parent has a weight problem, you have a 10 percent chance of developing one.

Some psychologists claim these odds exist because fat parents feed their children the same fattening things that they eat—pancakes and syrup in the mornings, fried foods, and rich desserts. The theorists say the link is *environment,* not heredity; it's how you were brought up that determines what you'll weigh. But that leads to a question: Why, in a family of three children with a fat mother, will only one turn out fat? The mother clearly feeds all three the same foods; why does only one gain weight?

The psychiatrists have an answer for that. The environment, they say, has a different impact on each child. The fat child will be:

1. the insecure child
2. the rejected child
3. the repressed child

And the list goes on. The bottom line, you see, is that shrinks get nervous when they run out of mothers to blame.

One of my patients, Jane, told me, "People always assume my mother stuffed me, and it couldn't be farther from the truth. My mother snatched food *away* from me, broiled everything, and allowed me only one candy bar a week." She sighed. "It didn't help."

The fact is, the primary underburner is *born,* not made. A Canadian study in the 1970s followed the growth of two hundred adopted children and found that the child's body type most often resembled the natural parents, not the adopted ones. A 1986 study of 540 adults in Denmark strongly echoed those results. This time, however, people were ready to listen, and the study has caused a furor.

It's funny though that even now, with overwhelming evidence in favor of genetics, the psychiatrists still refuse to back down. Overweight people, they insist, should not interpret these findings to mean it's all in the genes: "Fat people statistically have fat dogs," an expert told me recently, "and you can't blame that on the dogs' genes!" I admit I didn't have an answer for that—except, perhaps, that dogs will eat anything and everything you put under their noses, whereas kids eat only until they're full.

"And besides," he continued, "genetic fats can still display some willpower in their food intake." That's my least favorite term in the language: *willpower.* As if underburners ate everything they wanted. As if eating less than 2,000 calories a day—and *no* starchy, fatty foods— were as simple as passing up a second piece of cake.

No, I'm afraid the genetic underburner will have an uncomfortable relationship to food no matter what's in the cupboard. Having said that, it's time to admit that environment *can* make the problem better or worse and that once, as a nation, we only made things worse. Not so long ago, a baby's beauty was judged by the number of rolls of fat on his or her legs, and nutritionists told young mothers to plump those infants up. Many women found breast-feeding beneath their dignity and couldn't wait to shift the little ones to solid baby food, which invariably contained monstrous amounts of added sugar. If calories were all that really mattered, every American over twenty would be overweight. But a lot of kids came out thin. And, of course, we lauded their energy and *willpower.*

The good news, then, is that if you haven't inherited the tendency to be overweight, chances are you'll never be extremely fat, no matter what your environment is like. And you'll always be complimented on your willpower, even though you can eat far more than your underburning friends.

All babies must store fat for enormous growth, and so chubby babies do not necessarily mean fat adults. Some lost their baby fat in a few years; in others, it never goes away. As of now, we can't accurately predict which infants will have the genetic talent for manufacturing scores of new fat cells on a regular basis. That, by the way, is one thing that distinguishes an underburner from a mere overeater: The latter stuffs his or her existing fat cells to the limit (and is, at most, ten or fifteen pounds overweight); the former has the miraculous ability to increase the *number* of fat cells ad infinitum. And they don't go away.

The first reliable clue to the true underburner comes in the *latency* period, from age six to ten, when growth is slow and silent and most normal children have that lean, thin-legged, flat-tummied look. Underburners, on the other hand, tend to have convex abdomens, chubby thighs, and puffy little knock-knees. They eat more, huff and puff more, and have less muscle and muscle strength. (They're the ones who can't shimmy up the rope in gym class.) They have less coordination than *mesomorphs* (the muscular kids) and prefer bike-riding to running sports, softball to soccer. Unless they're already huge—and hence, tough to tackle—they're the last ones picked for a team. They all seem to love sweets. In a family of three, they're often outnumbered by two thin siblings, who eat more, move more, and are less preoccupied with foods containing sugar.

If left to their own devices, with no parental supervision, they can become quite obese, even before adolescence (age ten to age thirteen). At this stage, socioeconomic and ethnic factors play the biggest role in who, of the fat-prone, will be the fattest. In other words, if the family routinely eats a lot of pasta, fried chicken, or heavy desserts, it's hello Fat Albert. And if the kids are permitted to snack all the time and watch television for hours, they'll be bigger yet. TV has actually been cited in studies as one reason kids are heavier than ever; it helps keep them passive and sedentary, and they don't burn as many calories.

Since there's no real growth spurt in the latency period (that's why it's called latent), the excess fat means there's a deficiency in the mechanism regulating body weight. And right now there's nothing we can do to correct that; all we can change is the environment. That's what I did with Shawn.

Shawn, age ten, was one of the "key children"—kids who carry house keys because their parents are at work when school lets out. Most of her time she spent alone, with sitters, or with her older brothers, and every day she'd plop herself down in front of the TV set with a box of cookies, a bag of potato chips, and a soda. Her older brothers, all athletic and skinny, made constant fun of her weight, which just made her want to eat more. When I saw her for the first time she was five feet two inches and 230 pounds. It was a tragedy. Her parents, although concerned, were too busy trying to make ends meet; they neither helped nor understood their one fat-prone child. Luckily, the school social worker petitioned a sympathetic agency, which sent Shawn to me.

I wish I could have altered her genes on the spot, but alas, that's never an option. So the first step was to involve her entire family. I called them into my office and explained, as straightforwardly as I could, that Shawn was a different type of person than her brothers. Thinness was not *natural* for her. She'd have to work hard at it, and she'd need all the help from her family she could get. Once they realized that Shawn wasn't to blame for her problem, the entire family was surprisingly receptive. (Also, the stethoscope and white coat tend to awe people—doctors mean business.)

Then I called the physical education department of the school and asked them to work out a program of calisthenics geared to her needs. Initially, all they could get her to do were floor exercises: sit-ups, squat thrusts, jumping jacks. But ever so gradually they worked her into an aerobic regimen: jumping rope, swimming, jogging. Today, one year later, Shawn weighs 180 pounds and has grown three inches. That might not sound like a complete victory to you (she's still overweight), but given her age, background, and metabolism, it's a bloody miracle. At that weight, she can have a life.

I see many children from even less affluent homes than Shawn's, children at least thirty pounds overweight before they're ten years old. Think how difficult it is for an *adult* to lose thirty pounds, and you'll begin to understand the magnitude of the problem.

Puberty and Adolescence

After age ten, a deceptive time of life arrives: the pre-growth-spurt weight gain. In this phase, both sexes get chubby again in preparation for what may or may not be the most concentrated period of growth in their lives.

Young boys put on fat from ages eleven to fourteen in anticipation of their growth hormone, which the body begins to manufacture after age thirteen. With luck, this will help them shoot up to substantial heights. Growth hormone, as well as the sex hormone testosterone, is a very potent fat-burner, and most boys who gain weight at this time emerge both leaner and taller for it in a couple of years.

Adolescent male underburners don't have it so bad either. Their muscle mass, bone size, and hormones not only eat up their pre-growth-spurt fat but often absorb a lot of their baby and latency fat, too. So the male who starts out as an underburner—with too many fat cells—can spring into adulthood looking leaner than you'd have ever thought possible. Be warned, however, that his underburning tendency remains. The reformed male underburner will never be able to eat as much as his normalweight counterparts. But he's still lucky: He won't have a noticeable weight problem unless he takes in more than 4,000 calories a day. Compare this to female underburners, who can manufacture and maintain fat on as little as 2,000.

Mothers are always hoping for a magical height increase in their chubby daughters, but if the girl has started menstruating, there isn't going to be much. Heavier adolescent girls start their periods earlier (at ten or eleven) and their sex hormone, estrogen, is fat-*storing*. Unfortunately, the larger supply of estrogen turns off their fat-burning hormone and grinds their growth spurts to a halt. The cavalry doesn't come.

Once the fat-burning growth spurt stops and the estrogen arrives, it gets more difficult for females to keep thin. Estrogen, along with bad food habits—skipping meals, going on binges, and poor nutritional knowledge—makes females the fatter of teenagers. My greatest successes have come when girls are lucky enough to grow beyond five feet four inches. "You should see Linda!" a mother will tell me. "She's so thin now, thanks to you." Then I do see Linda, who has mercifully grown to five feet eight inches, and I silently thank Mother Nature for lending the doctor a hand. I wish she'd help me out more often.

Why Women Are More Likely to Be Underburners

Fact: Women are more likely than men to be heavy. Almost a quarter of them weigh at least 20 percent above what's considered normal for their build, while only 14 percent of men are similarly overweight. And the gap widens with age. At 65 years of age, 37 percent of all women are overweight, as opposed to 7 percent of men.

Why the disparity? The problem is women's bodies and what nature intends them to accomplish. Before puberty, girls (except underburners) have little excess body fat. When they begin to have periods, however, they suddenly find themselves with 10 to 15 percent more fat than men. The addition is the key to human existence: It means a girl can sustain a nine-month pregnancy and then breast-feed a baby for the early years of its life. After menstruation begins, nature is very protective of female fat. Try to lose it and you'll get a fight.

This resistant fat will sustain a woman through long periods of starvation, much longer than a man could survive. A woman on a hunger strike can live nine months—the time of an average pregnancy—while her male counterparts die in about two. (Women, however, are more likely to starve themselves for cosmetic rather than political reasons.)

Men are biologically designed to do one principal thing: Make women pregnant. For that they don't need much fat—enough for a few minutes of bump-and-grind. The woman, then, bears the real burden of perpetuating the species, and nature, not trusting the elements, has helped her out with the gift of fat. In our less desperate times, women have been trying to take the gift back, but this store has a "No Returns" policy. Which is why I like to give gift certificates.

Chapter 2

WHAT SHOULD UNDERBURNERS WEIGH?

Set-Point Weight Versus Goal Weight

My patients are always complaining that the last ten or fifteen pounds of a diet are impossible to lose. I've seen many successful dieters who, after losing thirty or forty pounds, can't drop another. I've seen them cry, swear, pound the wall next to the scale when it doesn't give them the news they want to hear, and storm out of my office. Sometimes they give up their diets in disgust, ignore my weight-maintenance program, and return to their original degree of heaviness in a couple of months. I've also seen more determined types exercise like demons and starve themselves down to a low-low weight they're incapable of holding. After a week or two of normal eating, they've gained those last pounds back.

What is this elusive target weight? Who sets it, and why?

A so-called goal weight is usually given to the hapless dieter by someone who has read an insurance company chart. The chart says that given a certain height and build, a person should weigh x number of pounds, plus or minus five. For example, a female twenty-five years or older, five feet three inches tall, should weigh 115 pounds, give or take five. This weight becomes the dieter's goal.

The chart has ruled for many years, but a lot of people—women in particular—can't get within spitting distance of their "goal" weight, no matter how much they exercise or starve. Most charts generously allow for differences in build, and so often a woman will turn to me and ask, hopefully, "Do you think I have a large build, doctor? Do you think I'm big-boned?" I look them up and down, clasp my fingers around their wrists, measure their shoulders, and say, "Well, at least a medium-large." Then they smile and feel better. I think I play the "I Must Have a Large Build" game every day.

It's not a very productive exercise, though, because it ignores the real issue: The goal weight is bogus. It's just the wrong concept, and it has destroyed more potentially successful diets than any other cause I know. The assumption that everyone who is the same height should weigh the same, give or take a little for differences in build, is preposterous. We can accept the idea that people the same height can have wildly different shoe (or, for that matter, breast) sizes, but we can't extend that concept to their weight.

Early in my practice, I was guilty of setting unreasonably low goal weights. My formula began with the assumption that a five-foot person should weigh one hundred pounds. For each additional inch, you add five pounds for women and seven pounds for men. So, I reasoned, a five-foot-three-inch female should weigh 115 pounds, plus or minus five. *Voilà*—the goal. Like many doctors and nutritionists, I was pretty obnoxious to patients who couldn't reach it. I thought they were cheating or else had "diet amnesia" from their starvation-induced fatigue. Eventually, my colleagues and I passed these unrealistic expectations on to the dieters themselves, and many have refused to relinquish them.

I don't know how I could have been so mulish. After all, I'm a perfect example of someone constantly frustrated by a "goal" weight. At five feet three inches and 130 pounds, I was called "pleasingly plump" and told that if I'd just lose ten pounds, I'd be magnificent. I went on many diets without success; finally, when I was twenty-five, working twenty hours a day as an intern and eating sporadically, I managed—*just* managed—to hit 118. For the first time in my life, I saw my kneecaps.

Alas, the period of starvation, sleeplessness, and racing the corridors of a ten-story hospital came to an end. When I became a psychiatric resident and had hour-long therapy sessions, regular meals, and endless staff meetings, my weight climbed back to 130 and my kneecaps disappeared. It wasn't so bad. The price of my magic 118 pounds had been chronic fatigue, hair loss, irregular periods, and a haggard look. The elusive 115 was never the right weight for me. At that age, the weight my body liked—*no matter who said I was "plump"*—was 130. I looked good at 130, I felt good at 130, and I wore a size nine at 130. Period. End of story.

Everyone has a weight at which—given normal eating patterns and a reasonable amount of exercise—their body levels off. More precisely, the body defends against any further loss. This is called the *set-point weight,* and it varies from person to person. It's usually determined by age twenty-five, and many people stay within a few pounds of it for life. Your set-point weight might not be the weight your mother, spouse, or employer deems perfect, but there's nothing you can do about that—it's *set.*

Well, there is an exception, and not a happy one. Underburners suffer from a "sliding" set point, and the slide is generally *up.* So after a major gain and a set-point advance, weight loss can be even more difficult. As I'll discuss in later chapters, there are specific periods in an underburner's life when his or her set point tends to slide, and it pays to be extravigilant when you're in one.

As I explain to some teenage girls today, that their ideal weight is ten or fifteen pounds higher than they think it should be, tears spring into their eyes. Many refuse to believe me. It's usually not until a woman is forty and has chased an impossible weight all her life that she finally agrees to reevaluate her goals. That's what happened to me.

Here is the formula I now use to devise a goal weight for the female underburner. The result should be close to the person's set-point weight.

Using the formula

$$\text{five feet} = 100 \text{ pounds}$$

in normalweight females add five pounds per inch. So

$$\text{five feet three inches} = 115 \text{ pounds}$$

For the underburner add 10 to 15 pounds at 25 years of age. So

$$115 + 15 = 130 \text{ pounds}$$

Then, to adjust for age, add about one pound a year to a maximum of fifteen pounds. A fifty-year-old underburner at this height could normally weigh 145 pounds. You should add another ten to fifteen pounds if the underburner has previously weighed as much as two hundred pounds; chances are that his or her set point has become fairly steep. So the set-point weight for a fifty-year-old underburner with a previous weight of 250 could be as high as 160. Repeated attempts to drop below that can lead to frustration, depression, and, yes, weight gain.

You'll be delighted to know that Metropolitan Life Insurance recently revised its tables to include a range of 110 to 147 pounds for women five feet three inches. Unfortunately, the chart doesn't take the critical age factor into account. Nor does it really help me explain to my patients why they all can't be 110 pounds if they want to be.

Chapter 3

UNDERBURNERS ARE DIFFERENT

The Normalweight Responds to Hunger;
Underburners Respond to Appetite and Hunger

Hunger is the biological drive that ensures that humans eat. Without it, people wouldn't always remember they needed nutrition, and sooner or later, down they'd go. End of species; *that's all, folks.* Logically, people have assumed that hunger is an accurate gauge of how much food you need to survive. If you burn 1,000 calories performing a task, the reasoning goes, you'll consume that many calories for dinner and won't be hungry any more. Human equilibrium: Energy consumed as food equals energy put out at work. Simplicity itself.

Only it's not so simple for underburners. They get the most out of every calorie, remember, so they don't need as much food as normalweights. If nature were perfect, underburners would be less hungry than their normalweight counterparts. But it appears they eat more because they are, in fact, hungrier—despite their enormous fat storage. It's almost as if nature forgets about their excessive energy stores and continues to concentrate on day-to-day survival.

What goes wrong? Failure of will has been the principal scapegoat, and, once again, the victim gets the blame. I'm reminded of a Germanic doctor who was in charge of a famous diet program that offered its prisoners extremely meager amounts of food. As one heavy woman carefully scraped the last bit of flesh from a grapefruit, he marched through the dining room, grabbed the fruit from her plate and flung it to the floor, shouting "Don't be such a pig!" The message was clear: "You've stuffed long enough! You shouldn't be eating at all!"

No one gets fat on grapefruit—not because it eats through flab, as dumb mail-order-diet ads suggest, but because it's low in calories and will never satisfy an underburner's cravings. Nor do underburners get so big on omelets and salad. Theirs is not a random, all-encompassing hunger; they don't binge on *anything.* They're very specific. In a famous experiment on humans, both fat and thin people were placed in a room for a long period of time. They were given a bland but nutritionally sound liquid supplement and instructed to drink as much as they needed to stay full. The fat people actually drank *less* of the liquid and they lost weight. The thin people, on the other hand, drank as much as they needed to maintain their weight.

Why don't underburners operate like that in real life? Obviously because the world is not made up of bland, liquid supplements, which don't trigger their appetites. Underburners have quite distinct food preferences, especially for what I call the *carbofats.*

Carbofats are the underburner's favorite—mucho fat attached to mucho carbohydrates, usually with heaps of sugar. You know them as "sweets:" cookies, cake, pie, candy. They're not to be confused with the *fatcarbos,* which are primarily fat with a carbohydrate base—gravy or cream sauces, macaroni and cheese. Fatcarbos can make you fatter, but they're not as dangerous to a diet. For underburners, it's the carbofats that are addictive, and the risk of bingeing with them is astonishingly high. Normalweights, on the other hand, have much more tolerance for both dreaded substances.

Research has shown that the underburners' elevated response has nothing chemically to do with their taste buds. Yes, they do enjoy the pleasurable components of carbofats, the sweetness, the richness, the crunchiness. But they also eat too many junky, fatty, less attractive meals, dubbed by researchers "cafeteria food." When scientists want rats to gain weight, they feed them cafeteria food; when they want rats to lose weight, they give them nutritionally balanced but boring chow. Underburners also overrespond to these combinations of fat and carbohydrates, and the presence of a "cafeteria diet" makes them overeat, too.

Hunger does not have to be a factor; what we're talking about here is *appetite,* which means a strong craving for a specific food—in this case fat, sugar, or chocolate. Our fat-laden society is flushing out more underburners than ever. Many fast-food restaurants fry burgers and potatoes in enormous quantities of grease; a meal at one of them can easily exceed 1,000 calories. So you see fierce cravings among people who, in a more healthful culture, wouldn't have a weight problem. Recently, I met a young woman with a "thing" for baked potatoes. Five years ago, no one would have thought twice about them, but with the advent of microwave ovens and fast-food baked potatoes, she averaged eight "fixes" a day. Had she settled for a plain potato, she wouldn't have gained much weight (or consumed as many); but she insisted on eating them with butter, cheese, bacon bits, and sour cream, all that fat turning an innocent carbohydrate into a dangerous carbofat. She gained, all right. And so have other fast-food freaks.

Baked-potato obsessions are relatively uncommon. The underburner's real Waterloo is the sugary carbofat, and that's why I won't introduce even small amounts into a reducing diet. That means *no* cookies, candy, or ice cream in *any* quantity. Sugar seems to trigger an urge for more sugar. No matter how long someone has been off the stuff, after one taste the habit returns with the same raging intensity.

It reminds me of the heroin addicts I used to treat as a resident in psychiatry. One patient, a young, attractive male, told me he mainlined because he was bored and depressed. But he knew how destructive his habit was—how it controlled his life, maimed his body, and ruined his work. He swore he'd never use drugs again. Then a young girlfriend came to visit. She was his supplier, we later learned, and drugs were her hold on him. He was intellectually and socially so far above her that the only way she figured she could keep him was by persuading him to go AWOL from the hospital and then reintroducing him to smack. When we found him, a mere seventy-two hours later, he was back on his six-bag-a-day habit. No more insight, no more resolutions. He was hooked and I was devastated.

Obviously, chocolate cookies aren't heroin (or even alcohol), but there's an odd resemblance to the underburner who breaks a diet. He comes into the office overweight and out of control, in a feeding frenzy, hooked on carbofats or fatcarbos, and hating himself. He says boredom, depression, or frustration make him eat, and he admits it's dumb to use food as an antidote to stress, particularly when the food is more destructive than the stress. He agrees to go cold turkey and to stop eating carbofats and fatcarbos. We "de-sweeten" him. He loses weight, grows more confident, and announces, "I'll never get fat again!" Christmas comes and his wife bakes lots of cakes and cookies. She says, "You've been so good. Just one taste won't hurt." (Pushers come in all shapes and sizes.) He tastes. And he is hooked again. *The Lost Weekend* with chocolate chip cookies.

For a long time physicians have hesitated to label food a physically addictive substance. It's not always evil—people must eat, after all, and food doesn't cause dramatic changes in consciousness or the ability to reason. But it can certainly change your size, mood, health, and self-image. It does not cost you your job, but it can cost you job opportunities. It can destroy a marriage (or prevent one). It doesn't kill you outright, but it does increase the risk factors that shorten your life, making you a likely candidate for heart disease.

How many times had I heard my patients say, "It's a good thing I'm not an alcoholic because I can't stop at one!"? Some joke—they're more aware of their problem than they realize. Only *their* substance is sugar. Not the natural sugar in sugarcane—where it's combined with impurities, pulp, and fiber—but the refined and concentrated stuff, powerful enough to trigger appetite and weight gain and even to lower their energy levels.

Why should carbofats cause such craving and bingeing? My hunch is that everyone has a *critical carbohydrate level* (or CCL), a level at which carbohydrates, in both normalweights and underburners, trigger intense cravings. I'm convinced that most underburners have an extremely low trigger point, much lower than normalweights have. In a famous experiment, normalweight volunteers were fed up to 8,000 calories a day to make them gain weight. These were men who had never before experienced cravings of any sort and whose normal calorie intake was about 3,500 to 4,000 calories a day. But lo, they suddenly reported sugar and carbohydrate cravings, even with all that food. *The elevated levels of carbohydrate triggered their high CCLs.* On massive amounts of sweets, they were behaving like underburners.

Right now there's nothing we can do about a low CCL except tiptoe around it. It can't be bargained with, it can't be reasoned with. Until we find a drug that will clamp onto the body's clamoring sugar receptors, the solution is *not to take the first bite,* especially when a second, third, and fourth are available. (I'm also convinced that someday we'll find chocolate receptors in most underburner's brains—the true chocoholic knows there's no substitute.)

One of the oddest statements that keeps surfacing in my office is, "Sweets don't bother me, but I crave salt—especially before my period." I used to accept this at face value, until I noticed my salt cravers weren't losing weight. Aside from a mild increase in the normal female's water retention, I couldn't figure out why this craving would cause so much trouble. So I investigated.

"Do you take salt in the palm of your hand and lick it?" I asked one.

"Oh, no!" came one horrified reply. "When I say I crave salt I mean pretzels, crackers, and potato chips."

Eureka. What they really craved was a salty carbofat or fatcarbo.

"So why not give them just one?" you ask. "What harm can one do?" Interesting question. A respected research team thinks that dieters' cravings should be treated with limited doses of carbohydrates to ease their pain. And behavioral psychologists—the ones who think that people go wrong because they haven't been properly *trained,* much like bad dogs—have been trying to teach underburners to stop at one cookie, one candy, one potato chip. The behaviorists equate bingeing with naughty, compulsive behavior and maintain that anyone can be taught to stop it. Lotsa luck, guys. There's a fascinating lawsuit in California now, prompted by some behaviorists who tried to teach recovered alcoholics to stop at one drink. They reintroduced the men to booze and triggered alcoholic binges. Too bad they never learn the lesson.

I think introducing carbofats or fatcarbos into a dieter's life on a daily basis spells disaster. Eat sugar and you are at risk. Once you taste it, expect your appetite for more to last at least two hours. Only time will diffuse those carbofat dreams, and most people binge before the cravings pass.

Underburners Gain Weight by Making New Fat Cells;
Normalweights Gain by Increasing the Size of Fat Cells

The point cannot be made often enough: People gain weight in two ways, one by increasing the size of their fat cells (we call this *hyper-*

trophic obesity), the other by increasing the number of fat cells in their body *(hyperplastic* obesity). The latter is by far the more dangerous: You can always make fat cells smaller, but you can't make them go away.

Normalweights, of course, have hypertrophic obesity, and that limits the amount of their weight gain to ten or twenty pounds. But underburners can increase the size *and* the number of their fat cells. No one knows why. Either underburners are born with a fixed amount of "prefat" cells, or the cells they've got have the ability when filled beyond a certain point to bud out a whole new set. Lose weight and those cells are still there, crying to be filled again.

Personalities have played too big a role in the treatment of obesity; there haven't been enough studies of the fat itself. (You don't just treat a disease by psychoanalyzing the person who has it.) How does the fat cell survive? Does it have its own intelligence? The more you diet, the more resistant it gets to destruction—which suggests that it does, indeed, know how to take care of itself. The fat cell is so tough that blockages that would spell death for the brain, heart, and muscle do not seem to hurt it at all.

We're now learning about different types of fat in humans. One of the most intriguing (although unreported) papers to come out of the Fourth International Congress on Obesity was by a group of Scandinavian researchers who divided fat into two types: stable and labile. Fat deposits in the abdomen, they said, were easily tapped for energy, the first deposits to be burned (hence *labile,* or liable to change). The fat around the hips and thighs, on the other hand, was stable and never seemed to be raided.

The stable fat is more characteristic of females, and in the researchers' experience (as well as mine), it doesn't respond well to diet, exercise, or massage. This might also be the "gatekeeper fat," which directs the placement and amount of all other fat. Who knows? If we can figure out how it works (and how to make it go away), we could lick obesity in a couple of decades. Sounds good to me.

Normalweights Have One Set Point; Underburners Can Create New Set Points

As I suggested in the chapter on set-point versus goal weight, normal-weights have a fixed set point. They might gain that ten or twenty pounds, but they'll return to their set-point weight when they correct their eating habits or start running five miles a day. On the other hand, once underburners gain a lot of weight, their set point can slide up, up, up. This is called a "sliding lipostat," or the "rachet effect." (Rachets can go forward, but not back.) After a diet, there's a tremendous biological tug back to that set point; about all you can do to fight it is diet some more; do frequent aerobic exercise; start smoking (dumb, but it does speed up your metabolism); take diet pills (ouch!); and sometimes, if you're rich and gung-ho enough, arrange for lipo-suction surgery, a procedure whereby fat can actually be broken up and sucked out of the thighs and buttocks.

Underburners Don't Feel Full After a Meal Without Carbofats; Normalweights Can Feel Full After Any Large Feeding

It's true: Give an underburner a big meal with a steak and salad, and you'll get an underburner poking around for *something* half an hour later. On further inquiry, that something will turn out to be a carbofat, although a straight sugar or starch will often satisfy. We've fed the stomach, but frustrated the eager carbohydrate receptors. You see the same problem with alcoholics and alcohol. Fortunately, there are ways of satisfying those pesky carbohydrate receptors that don't necessarily trigger a binge. Which brings us to the following sad fact.

Underburners Binge; Normalweights Eat Normally

Underburners of all ages and normalweight female teenagers binge. In fact, their binges are so frequent that fat people were once considered clinically bonkers. Actually, anyone who severely reduces his or her calories—even normalweights on a particularly brutal fast—can set themselves up for a binge.

The biological attempt of the binge is for the body to reopen closed fat cells—to maintain, if you will, the status quo. Its object is always highly palatable, high-caloric-density foodstuffs, which means as many calories as possible packed into the smallest possible space. Which means carbofats or fatcarbos. Chocolate cake to you. By the time the binge has been stopped (sometimes by sickness), you've gained back lost weight fast—an unfair amount of weight, really, because it's never proportional to the amount of food actually eaten. A binge might represent only 3,000 or 4,000 calories, which is one to one-and-a-third pounds of fat, but the poor underburning binger can emerge with a scale weight as much as six pounds higher.

Why the injustice? One reason is that carbos attract water, so water weight comes back quickly. Another has to do with a high level of something called lipoprotein lipase, an enzyme that makes it easier to refill your fat cells. After a diet, the underburner's lipo level stays high instead of dropping down, as it does in normalweights. So you need far fewer calories to make a pound of fat—sometimes as little as (it breaks my heart to give you this figure) 800 calories.

In practical terms, the cycle goes like this:

A calorie-restrictive diet leads to
Loss of weight.

Loss of weight leads to
Hunger and cravings.

Hunger and cravings lead to
A taste of the forbidden food.

A taste of the forbidden food leads to
"Can't eat just one" and more forbidden food.

More forbidden food leads to
Your Critical Carbohydrate Level—surpassed!

Surpassing your CCL leads to
The Binge.

The Binge leads to
A fast refilling of your fat cells.

A fast refilling of your fat cells leads to
A mess of brand-new baby fat cells.

Brand-new baby fat cells lead to
Higher weight gain.

Higher weight gain leads to
Guess what?
A calorie-restrictive diet!

And here we go again, only it gets tougher every time. As you can see, this cycle isn't the result of psychological aberrations. It's *biologically programmed.*

Can science interrupt this awful process? It hasn't really tried. Our understanding of obesity has been set back fifty years by the medical specialty that also set back the treatment of depression, schizophrenia, and anxiety—psychiatry.

By the blind insistence that fat is a psychological problem and not a disease, millions of research dollars have been flushed down the drain in search of that elusive repressed sexual urge or traumatic early childhood experience that makes people eat more than they should.

Fortunately—finally—that era is over. Medicine is now on the right, metabolic track.

Underburners Don't Fill Up as Quickly as Normalweights

I'm certain that underburners have a larger capacity than normalweights. Probably their stomachs can expand more, and so more food goes in before the brain is signaled: "Hey, no more, I'm full!" (Stomach reductions—a radical operation that some very obese people resort to—reduce the amount of food they want to eat.) Underburners like bigger portions of even the so-called "right food"—not just carbofats.

Behaviorists keep clanging their bells and yelling, "Portion control! Portion control!" which is their term for limiting patients to teeny-tiny portions and training them to believe that "one is enough."

I recently had a nasty disagreement about portion control with nutritionists at a diet camp where I'm a medical consultant. The campers are on a tough, 1,200-calorie diet that includes a salad bar at lunch and dinner. They have a strenuous exercise program, so there's no question they're burning calories like crazy when they sit down to eat; they're also quite hungry. The nutritionists demanded the kids learn that one serving of salad per meal is sufficient. I felt they should be allowed as much lettuce as they wanted.

"These are hungry kids," I said, "and they'll always be hungry kids. They have to learn to eat things that will fill them up but keep them from gaining weight. Salad is one of the few foods that will do that."

I won my point, but the nutritionists got even. They made the salad plates so small and the tongs so difficult to maneuver that getting even a modest amount of greens was impossible. You had to make three or four trips.

The problem with portion control is that some arbitrary and usually thin authority decides what constitutes an adequate portion. It's like someone telling you that you should have sexual intercourse 2.6 times per week because that's the national average, and if you have less, you're frigid, and if you have more, you're oversexed. The idea of someone imposing what he or she thinks are correct portions interferes with your basic right to choose. It assumes that because you're overweight, your portions are too big. It's treating you like a child. And often that makes you *feel* like a child and maybe act like a child. So when the parents are away . . .

I hate to admit it, but portion control does have its uses in regard to dangerous foods, especially complex carbohydrates. Many underburners do have to go around with their carbohydrate receptors semistarved to achieve the kind of thinness they want, and a ceiling on how much you can eat might be the only thing that will work. I just object to the theory of it for *all* foods *all* the time. And more than that, I object to the attitude.

Underburners Eat More When They're Depressed (and Gain); Normalweights Eat Less (and Lose)

One of the things a true depression is supposed to do is kill your appetite. That's the theory, anyway, and shrinks stand by it. But when I was training in psychiatry, I had a number of depressed patients who actually gained weight. One of my superiors used to say—psychiatrists, you understand, are never without an answer—"That's simple: they're not really depressed."

"But they *are,*" I'd say. "They are extremely depressed."

"Do they have trouble sleeping?"

"Yes."

"Do they wake up early?"

"Yes."

"Sense of emptiness?"

"Yes."

"Withdrawn, fatigued, difficulty thinking and talking?"

"Yes, yes, yes."

"Loss of appetite?"

"No."

"Well, then it's not a true depression."

"So what is it?"

Pause.

"Self-indulgence."

I would have strangled him, but they'd have labeled me a hysterical paranoid with homicidal tendencies, and I'd never have been allowed to see my, yes, *clinically depressed* patients again.

The reason my patients gained weight was because they were underburners, and underburners eat when they're depressed. They don't eat because they're lonely and unhappy and need oral gratification, which is why shrinks tell you all fat people eat. They eat because they no longer have the psychological energy to keep from eating.

Understand this: In every underburner there resides a much fatter one. But society—which is quick to label them "gluttons"—impels them to live in a state of semistarvation. They reduce their weight to below the level at which they can maintain it without effort—that is, their unusually high set point. Yes, underburners can be overweight in relation to the rest of the population, yet underweight in relation to their own set point. The result is that their bodies exert a constant pressure on them to eat and gain weight. Strong, mentally healthy underburners fight a daily battle to keep from consuming those calories. But when they're depressed, they don't have that extra energy. They're not gluttons, they're just too tired to fight anymore. They cooperate with their bodies. If eating actually does make them feel better, you can understand why: Who wants to spend a lifetime at war with one's body?

It's a battle normalweights almost never have to fight. In fact, normalweights often have to remind themselves to eat. They forget the time of day, they miss meals. When they're depressed, they're also too tired to fight, only that means they *don't* eat. And, of course, the pounds fall off.

Chapter 4

BRINGING UP BABY

And Keeping His Weight Down

Few things in my office make my blood boil like a heavy mother who pacifies her restless child with a cookie. After all, underburners don't always generate fat cells in a vacuum. "What are you feeding him?" I ask, scarcely concealing my horror. "How could you dream of plying your child with cookies?" The replies are as varied as they are senseless: "He didn't eat breakfast"; "He doesn't eat many sweets"; "It keeps him from driving me crazy"; "He doesn't have a weight problem."

Famous last words.

It's no easy job raising an underburner: You're damned if you feed, and you're damned if you hold food back. Figuring out which to do (and when to do it) is the toughest lesson of all. And the most vital. Although genes play the strongest role in the shape an underburner assumes, his weight can be profoundly influenced by home environment and by his parents' concern with health, diet, and exercise. If a fat-prone child is placed in a home that encourages thinness, he probably won't manifest his fat trait early in life. If, on the other hand, a fat-prone child is overfed by his family, he won't just get fatter earlier, but his fatness will be harder to combat.

Let's look at the evolution of two children, both genetically programmed to be heavy. We'll call them Andy and Bert.

Andy is breast-fed. That's a good way to limit infant weight, since babies don't overfeed themselves. Andy's parents delay solid food for six months, and when they do introduce it, they make sure it's natural. That means *no added sugar*. Some researchers suggest that early acquaintance with sugar (most baby foods are loaded with it) helps trigger a preference for sweets, which is reason enough to be very careful of what goes into your baby's mouth. (Although, let's be realistic, no matter when sugar is introduced, most kids love it. What you *can* control is early overeating.)

The slim environment also encourages eating at regular intervals, and snacks that are high in fiber and low in calories—fruits instead of candy, for example. A peanut-butter sandwich is served on whole-wheat bread without jelly, and fruit juice (often diluted) replaces soda. No one insists that Andy finish a meal he's had his fill of; no one uses ice cream as a reward for gobbling down the last of the liver or broccoli. The slim family loves exercise, teaches skills early (Andy gets his first tennis lesson at age four), and takes active vacations.

Now let's look at Bert, who has the hard luck to be born into a loving but misguided family. Bert is bottle-fed, so it's relatively easy to stuff a little more into him than he wants or needs. He snacks on high-fat and high-sugar sweets, which his parents use to quiet him down, console him, and, of course, reward him. He learns the adult habit of munching in front of the TV set. The cookie jar is never empty, and his family truly believes that baking an apple pie is a gesture of love.

Both Andy and Bert might be overweight by age two, but Bert will be much fatter. Andy will be at his biological set point, slightly heavier than normal, but certainly not obese.

What happens if a thin child is born into a fat-making environment? His body type, metabolism, increased energy, and natural food preferences will still encourage thinness. A popular myth about thin children is that they're so active they burn off all their fat as energy. But it's nature—not nurture—that's really responsible.

The Small Ones (Ages Two to Six)

Mothers always ask me how they can stop the seemingly inevitable weight gain in their chubby kids without doing psychological harm.

After all, the act of denying one's young children food can be very traumatic.

First, I tell them to relax a little and try not to let their children sense their panic. The very young child does not understand the consequences of being chubby or even the concept of fatness; nor can he concern himself with a diet for more than one meal at a time. The message you send to young children should be: *Eat healthy.*

The child incorporates this reasoning into his intellectual framework without necessarily understanding it. Call it brainwashing.

You'd be surprised at how this form of diet catechism sticks, even with a very young child. One of my health-conscious friends had a normalweight three-year-old with a severe viral illness. His appetite was poor, and his weight had dropped so alarmingly that his pediatrician said, "Feed him junk, just so he'll get some nourishment into his system." So his mother reluctantly bought him a milk shake at a local fast-food outlet. His eyes lit up with pleasure and he drank enthusiastically. Then, suddenly, he pushed it away.

"What's the matter?" asked his mother, alarmed.

"It's dessert," he whined. "I can't have dessert—I haven't eaten supper!"

Talk about *programmed.*

Another way to teach healthful eating is simply not to keep dangerous foods in the house—no cookies, potato chips, or ice cream. Don't worry about your normalweights; they'll live. Mothers and fathers often protest this advice, announcing, "There are other people who live in this house. Thin people. Why should they be made to suffer?"

I ask them one question: "If one of your children was an alcoholic, would you put a bottle of booze on the table because the other family members have a right to drink?" That usually shuts them up.

"Children can be taught to stop at one," some parents insist. Sure, you can teach your normalweights to stop at one but not your underburners. That box of cookies in the drawer will beckon day and night, crying to be finished. At this age you still have the authority to *provide* only one. Take advantage of it.

I have a thin, beautiful friend who lives on skim milk and cottage cheese but has a daughter who's built like her chunky father. The child had a humongous appetite from the minute she was born and, throughout her formative years, a food battle raged between her and her mother. My friend remained merciless, however, and every time the chubby little hand went out, she clapped down a celery or carrot stick. If she was feeling generous, she dispensed sliced apples or oranges, and sometimes even a plain bread stick. It worked. Today her fat-prone daughter is acceptably thin and is able to take over her food monitoring herself.

It wasn't pleasant, that ordeal, but the alternatives in this society are worse—a lonely and excluded teenage girl who might finally make food her principal consolation.

The Medium Ones (Ages Six to Ten)

This is called the latency period. It comes after the accelerated early growth and before the adolescent spurt. Nothing much is supposed to happen, either physically or emotionally—it's the calm before the storm.

I used to think this age was a little too young to begin serious talks about weight control, but I changed my mind after reading about normalweight fourth-grade girls on bona-fide weight-reduction diets. Earlier and earlier, it seems, children are forming their prejudices and values about weight, and so they respond extremely well to information and advice. This is a good time to offer alternatives to fattening foods and to stress regular meal habits, physical activity, and good health. It's also a time to encourage the underburner to be out and about in the world and not cooped up indoors in isolation.

I always have been a firm believer in underburners carrying their lunches to school: lunches that include a simple sandwich on whole-wheat bread, vegetables, and fruit. A hungry child can get more satisfaction on fewer calories in an intelligently packed cold lunch than in a fat-packed hot one.

This is the time to broaden your child's food base. He might hate string beans, until he eats them Chinese style, tossed in a wok with some ginger, garlic, and soy sauce. Ditto broccoli. I once had a patient who only ate meat, french fries, apples, and popcorn. The combination made her heavy, but it was, "Sorry, doc, that's all I eat," when she came in for a diet. I did my damnedest to concoct an apple-meat diet, but what could I do? The regime was too boring. Obviously, she's an extreme case, but the more low-calorie foods a person likes, the more variety is possible in a diet. And that could make the difference between sloggling on and throwing it all away.

Children get very hungry after school, so pay attention to afternoon snacks. Try to keep them low in calories (under 100) so they don't turn into regular mini-meals. A rice cake with a teaspoon of peanut butter is only 69 calories; and with a four-ounce glass of skim milk, it's about 100. One cookie can be 100 calories. Be careful of fruit juice and dried fruit. No underburner needs straight fruit juice—it has too much concentrated sugar. Dilute it. And dried fruit packs a lot of calories into a very small space. A small box of raisins is only 60 calories, but will it satisfy? Why not a bunch of grapes instead?

Another fact of life at this age is the fast-food restaurant. McDonald's, Wendy's, and their ilk are such a part of our culture that many kids feel deprived if they don't get to go. The problem is that most of this food contains staggering amounts of fat; some restaurants deep-fry their burgers as well as their french fries. One defense is to ask for a calorie chart of the various sandwiches served. (Most chains will supply you with one.) Then choose the chain—and the sandwich—that poses the least significant threat. Or, if your underburner can stand it, gently direct him toward the salad bar.

Perhaps, most important, this is the time to push physical activity. Not unrealistic physical activity, but something the child stands a decent chance of mastering. Otherwise, you can turn the kid off exercise for life. My mother made me tap dance, for instance, and I was a disaster. In my nightmares, I still see myself in a short little taffeta skirt, bouncing up and down, *thump, thump, thump.* Excruciating. No wonder I never pursued any sport. On the other hand, I'd have made a great goalie on the field-hockey team, but that option wasn't available then.

The Adolescent (Ages Ten to Thirteen)

The soft sell is over; it's time to get down to business. By now, a fat child realizes that he or she is different. The next step is an honest, unhysterical discussion of the problem. Unfortunately, this is a time of emerging sexuality, so the child has to deal with a hormonal storm as well as a weight problem. What's essential to have is a total body talk.

The fat body talk is as crucial as the birds and the bees and should be given the same time, respect, and privacy. You should use it to explore options together, but it's up to the adolescent to decide whether to take action. You can get a child to listen, but you can't force him or her to diet. I have had parents drag unwilling adolescents into my office and the results have been appalling. One cried for an entire hour; another left my office and was spotted thereafter at the local snack bar devouring a club sandwich, a milk shake, and a piece of pie.

So if you initiate the conversation and it elicits a sullen glance or pout, stop and resume in a few months. The underburner who ignores your helping hand is not yet ready to act; besides, there's a chance he'll come to you next time, having considered the problem in private. Constant pressure at this point can destroy a mother/daughter relationship, especially if the mother is thin and the daughter is chubby. Strangely enough, fathers and daughters don't breed the same hostility in this situation.

If the child is responsive, however, this is the perfect time to begin a program of weight control. That doesn't necessarily mean a weight-loss diet, just reduced intake to prevent weight *gain*. Education will make a difference now; this is still the age of reason.

The Teenager

Welcome to the age of unreason.

The sexes diverge. No more unisex—boys become men and girls become women. If you've been successful in raising and educating your male underburner, he'll be an okay weight and be able to eat 3,500 to 4,500 calories a day without gaining. This is because the combination of growth hormone and testosterone allows even the underburning male to be reasonably thin at this time of life.

However, the female underburner seems to have forgotten every nutritional lesson you taught her. She has discovered that if she doesn't eat at all, she isn't hungry. So she starves herself. No joke, half my office hours are spent arguing with female teenagers who think the perfect way to diet is simply to fast, and they get angry when I tell them they're dangerously wrong.

After the fasting ends, of course, the teenager goes on a binge, because *that's* the biological conclusion to starvation.

She sleeps a lot, also. Why? It's probably the combination of a crazy diet, emerging hormones (estrogen and progesterone), and just being an underburner and having a sluggish metabolism that makes her constantly tired.

She's angry at her parents because she has to be angry at someone for her weight. She's miserable because it's hard to be fat anytime, but when you're a teenager, it's hell.

The answer for you is to ride it out. Love her, support her, have diet foods and a diet plan available for her, and concentrate on convincing her of her total worth as a person. Encourage her talents, encourage her to exercise, and, if her studies won't suffer, encourage her to look for an after-school job—anything not associated with food. Even if she doesn't eat the pizza or donuts or fries, she'll be constantly tempted. I work with dieting patients all day, and even when I talk about blah weight-loss diets, I make myself hungry.

The sweet girl you knew as an adolescent will return, and with luck, she won't have done too much damage to herself. In the meantime, back off. Pressure, threats, and bribery will do no good. "But I just want you to be happy!" will do no good. All you can do is watch and wait.

School and the Underburner

Can schools help in the care and feeding of underburners? Absolutely, but they've been slow to respond to the overweight person's needs. I can't tell you how many times I've had to argue strenuously for the right of a child simply to *bring* a lunch. Schools have stubbornly refused to give up traditional high-calorie, loaded-with-fat favorites and explore a leaner approach to eating. They're in the marketplace like everyone else and feel that foods like pizza, spaghetti, and ice cream stand the best chance of being purchased by children. They wouldn't even consider skim milk as an alternative until the government's 1978 publication of "Dietary Goals for the United States," which advised Americans to consume less salt, sugar, and fat in their diets.

I'm sorry to report that what's known as a "salad" in many cafeteria lines still means an unidentifiable substance heavily laced with mayonnaise. Baked fish, which sounds good, still sits in a pool of congealed fat. Chicken will more often be served a la "tetrazini"—in a glutinous cream sauce—than simply broiled or baked. And macaroni and cheese continues to make a fast, cheap, out-of-the-can staple.

I don't think school menus need a 100 percent overhaul—let those with slim builds and good genes eat all the fat and sugar they can handle. But give the underburner a choice. Let him go through the cafeteria line and find a dish that's as appetizing as the food he's passing up. Consider this:

A small can of tuna surrounded by colorful raw vegetables	Instead of	Tuna salad with mayonnaise
1 or 2 hardboiled eggs 2 Rye Crisp crackers carrot sticks	Instead of	Egg salad with mayonnaise
An open-face sandwich with melted cheese and tomato on thin whole-wheat bread	Instead of	Pizza (same ingredients except oil)

Physical Education

The underburner is not a limber kid and often cannot run as fast, climb as high, or bend as well as normalweights. In more competitive team sports, he's the last to get picked, which makes for trauma even in stiff-upper-lip types. The school should recognize this trauma and should provide options for these exceptional students, options that make allowances for limitations in speed and agility.

Underburners aren't always phys. ed. washouts. They often have strength, endurance, and tenacity, qualities that go far in volleyball, long-distance running, biking, swimming, and guarding the goal in hockey. The underburner loves biking and swimming especially, where the wheel and the water do a lot of the work. But that's okay, because it's still aerobic exercise, and the underburner *enjoys* it. Even bird-watching is a plus for some of these kids if it encourages them to wander around outside instead of sprawling in front of the television.

I have seen many kids who needed the exercise turned off to physical fitness by indifferent, insensitive, and occasionally cruel gym instructors. Later, as adults, they often discover a sport they really love and can excel in. Too bad they missed out when it would have mattered the most.

Chapter 5

EATING DISORDERS

The Diets That Can Kill

No discussion of the early years of underburners would be complete without including *anorexia nervosa* and *bulimia,* the infamous teenage eating disorders. Too bad.

Anorexia

Anorexia is a condition in which young people, usually female, diet to the point of starvation and even death. While she's starving, the anorexic behaves as if she's on a normal diet. The only difference is that the diet moves beyond the point of reasonable thinness, until the dieter achieves the proportions of a skeleton. Instead of being alarmed by her appearance, the young woman refuses to believe she is too thin. She pinches tiny rolls of skin and claims they're flab. And she continues to diet.

Where is her family while all this is happening? To a point, they're watching and approving a successful diet—until they realize it's gone too far. Then they try to stop her, but the anorexic continues to starve. Sometimes they call in a therapist to stop her, but still the anorexic continues to starve. The therapist tries to figure out *why* the young woman would abuse herself this way; and the anorexic continues to starve. Talk and talk and more talk, while the "diet" progresses inexorably.

This is why anorexia has been called "the 'die' in dieting." While the family, the therapist, and the world watch and interpret, a young woman dies. What a waste. Psychiatric problems or not, no one in this day and age should die from acute vitamin deficiency or malnutrition associated with anorexia.

Although Ashley almost did.

Ashley, age fifteen, was brought to my office by her nervous, solicitous mother, a woman clearly frightened of her own daughter. The girl had been a normal, slightly rounded teenage underburner who'd gone on a weight-loss diet and had somehow forgotten to stop. Now, at five-feet-four-inches and 89 pounds, she looked less than healthy. Her skin was pallid, her eyes were sunken, her lips were cracked. But she was still pretty spunky. She even had the wit to hide two two-pound weights in the pockets of her jeans to make her weigh more. When I inquired about the bulges in her hips, she was quick to say they were wads of tissues.

"You could hurt your nose with these," I said, extracting them.

"Oh, them!" Ashley tossed off. "I forgot about *them!*"

Correction on the above weight: Ashley was 85 pounds. And dropping.

After examining the girl to assure myself she was, indeed, alive, I asked Ashley's mother why she'd brought her daughter for a consultation. I was a weight-loss doctor, after all, and Ashley seemed to be doing quite well on her own.

"We want you to regulate Ashley's diet," her mother said.

"She doesn't look like she's had much of any diet," I said.

"But she's agreed to start one," her mother insisted, with enthusiasm. "She's agreed to drink three meals of liquid protein a day."

"Three meals of liquid protein is a starvation diet!" I gasped.

"Yes, but it's so much more than she has been eating."

There was a pause to let all this sink in.

"Who is the 'we,' " I asked, "as in, 'We want you to regulate Ashley's diet'?"

"Oh, my husband and I. Ashley's therapist."

"You're telling me a therapist has been watching this child starve herself?"

"Yes, she's been helping Ashley with her problem!"

I thought I'd have a stroke on the spot. Suddenly, all I saw were the thousands of young anorexics dying useless deaths because no one was willing to take decisive action. This girl wasn't starving herself in private. She was starving herself under a therapist's care. And she was *delusional.* You don't reason with a dying, delusional young girl. You hospitalize her.

As calmly as possible, I told Ashley's mother that she was sitting on a keg of dynamite. I told her I'd known many anorexics who teetered on the brink of death for months and then suddenly failed so rapidly that not even the most heroic medical methods could save them. I told her that we'd have to find an internist who'd have Ashley admitted to the *medical* (not psychiatric) ward of the nearest hospital. "When her weight is above one hundred pounds," I said, "and her life is no longer in danger, she can have all the psychiatrists and diet doctors she wants." Luxuries mean more when you're alive.

Mother and daughter looked at me as if I'd gone mad.

The next day, I got a call from a woman who identified herself as Ashley's therapist.

"Do you remember what you told Ashley and her mother yesterday?" she asked.

"I certainly do."

"Well," she said, "don't you think that will destroy the therapeutic relationship?"

"I hope so!" I replied.

Ashley was hospitalized that day and "refed," at first by tube and then by mouth. Refeeding ceased at the weight of 105.

Ashley continued her psychotherapy. There were real problems there, and aside from the fact that she'd been dying, the treatment was slowly progressing. Now, however, a family doctor was weighing her every week to make sure her weight did not dip below one hundred pounds. Everybody was happy with the arrangement. Even Ashley.

Unfortunately, not all anorexic stories end this way. But the treatment of anorexia has progressed. Hospitalization and refeeding are now an integral part of the program. Then you have all the time in the world to deal with a troubled psyche.

What of that psyche? What drives a girl to become an anorexic? In some cases, it's a fear of growing up and facing her own sexuality. In others, it's the mind's attempt to take control of an uncooperative body.

Often, it's an attempt to get back at someone (a parent, perhaps) who has hurt the anorexic—the destructive impulse, unfortunately, turned on the victim herself. (Remember the jingle, "Someday I'll eat worms then I'll die, and you'll be sorry you made me cry!"?)

What interests me more is why this is a primarily female disease and why society—meaning friends, family, and professionals—let it go so far.

The problem is a cultural weight obsession that demands a woman be thinner than she often naturally can be, an obsession that bears the stamp of society's approval for females of any age on any diet.

Luckily, most adolescents don't have the resources to carry a weight-loss diet to starvation. However, when a teenager is a little more confused or alienated, or in the case of a particularly traumatic turn of events (a family or romantic crisis), a simple weight-loss diet can go haywire.

This does not happen when society does not let it happen. This does not happen to young men.

A California college physician told me a story about highly motivated and athletic freshman males. Without moms to supply regular meals, a few get feverishly caught up in physical training and studies and forget to eat. At this point, the athlete's buddies accompany him to the dining hall, where they make sure he has sufficient nourishment until this dangerous phase passes and he begins to eat regularly.

What a different story with a female. A dieting freshman comes to school forewarned about the Freshman Fifteen—that automatic fifteen pounds that freshman girls seem to gain from an increase in carbofats and late-night stuffing. So she diets, and the thinner she gets the more her peers approve. Maybe, if she's an anorexic, she reaches the delusional state that starvation and metabolic changes trigger. No one stops her. No one accompanies her to the dining hall and makes her eat. It's just a normal phase of female development.

In *Eating and Its Disorders,* Susan and Armond Wooly ask, very sensibly, "Would things be different if our hospitals and clinics were filled with young men whose educations and careers were arrested by the onset of anorexia nervosa, bulimia, or the need to make dieting and body-shaping exercise a full-time pursuit?"

How do the underburners specifically fit into the anorexia picture? Teenage female underburners are always on a diet, and this puts them in a high-risk category. Sometimes it's very difficult to distinguish a successful fanatic dieter, which you have to be if you're an underburner, from a potential anorexic. It becomes even more difficult when you consider that over 50 percent of young women entering college exhibit the anorexiclike behavior of starvation, bingeing, and purging (vomiting).

In my book *The Woman Doctor's Guide to Teen-Age Girls*, I said I didn't think normal kids became anorexic—there had to be a marked personality disturbance that was present before the anorexic episode. Now I think I was too optimistic. Given the right timing and the right set of circumstances, many of today's young women can have bouts of anorexia, and starvation and hormonal changes drive out whatever rationality they once possessed.

I have a checklist that will prove useful in distinguishing the normal dieter from the anorexic. But remember, normal dieters can come disturbingly close to anorexic behavior, and so it's a good idea to watch any young female who is dieting, especially if she seems unhappy or depressed.

Anorexic

1. Usually only mildly overweight, if overweight at all.

2. Extremely sensitive about any remarks about weight.

3. Allows seemingly minor fluctuations in weight to get in the way of doing things and going places.

4. Feels the reason people don't like her is connected to her weight.

Normal Dieter

1. Mild to severe overweight.

2. Varies from being slightly sensitive to taking it with a grain of salt.

3. Usually will go places if she can find something to wear. Goes to the beach, but doesn't wear a bathing suit.

4. Feels her weight does not influence the way people feel about her, especially other girls.

5. Exercises and moves constantly, sometimes at a frantic pace.	5. Difficult to get moving.
6. Loves dieting and enjoys being very thin. Preoccupied with weight.	6. Hates dieting. Feels angry at the world for having to diet.
7. Will vomit and take laxatives to feel thin.	7. Rarely vomits unless she is sick.
8. Periods stop.	8. Periods usually remain the same. Sometimes they become irregular or change their character as normal weight is approached.
9. Depressed or preoccupied.	9. Personality stays the same.

Bulimia

The psychiatric handbook defines bulimia as recurrent episodes of bingeing and purging. This translates as eating a lot of food in a short, fixed amount of time (usually less than two hours) and making yourself throw it up. The practice is so common that I'm surprised there aren't more unofficial freshman seminars in bulimia—Vomiting 101, say, or Advanced Principles of Gagging. Why shouldn't it be common? You can eat your cake and purge it, too. No wonder it's the most popular method for teenage girls to control their weight.

Sound horrible? Sound sick? Why? When normal adults take mystery pills and diuretics; pay thousands of dollars to starvation spas; go on absurd fruit-and-vegetable or rice-and-water diets; and submit to such drastic procedures as jaw-wiring, intestinal bypasses, stomach stapling, gastric balloons, and fat suctioning, I frankly don't find bulimia so shocking. Millions of teenage girls, plagued with images of thin, desirable women, find it the logical, if messy, solution to a depressing fact of life: That in a land of luscious, tempting foods, they must constantly deny themselves what others can frequently have.

Underburners are forced to live in a state of caloric deprivation to keep their weights at acceptable social levels. Acceptable social levels, however, might not be the same as acceptable biological weight. So they're always hungry, sometimes starving; and when you're starving, the corrective binge is a biological fact of life. After the binge, the vomiting—the fail-safe mechanism to prevent weight gain.

It's not harmless, though. The act of forcing up your stomach's contents on a regular basis can do a lot of damage; those digestive juices are heavily laced with acids. For starters, you can burn away the lining of your esophagus, the tube that connects the mouth to the stomach. You can also ruin the tone of the esophageal sphincter, which is the cap that keeps the stomach acids from spilling into the rest of your gut. The steady flow of acid can wear away the enamel on your teeth. Finally, throwing up your food means massive electrolyte losses: along with all those calories, you deplete your body of potassium, sodium, and fluids.

For the most part, this is another female-only syndrome. No, it's not a deep-seated psychological problem, stemming from depression and unfulfilled infantile needs. There's been a lot of hooey about bulimia and female masochism, about rewarding oneself and then feeling soiled and unworthy—and hence the purge. But show me a woman who can eat all she wants and not gain a pound, and I'll show you a woman who won't force herself to throw up.

Bulimia is a cultural problem, nurtured by a two-faced society that encourages us to eat but threatens us to stay thin. For underburners in particular, this is an impossible task. After a tough day on the job, they have to teach themselves *not* to think, "And now it's Miller Time."

Will the choice always have to be food or approval? Will our society ever stop subjecting females to this kind of torture? As long as we enforce impossible weight standards for women and refuse to encourage their sense of self-worth on the basis of who they are, not how they look, we will ignore the true dynamics of their rebellion. And we'll look the other way while they throw up.

Chapter 6

BECOMING AN UNDERBURNER

It Can Happen Here

We have discussed the born underburners, who represent the most serious obesity problem in our country. But there are just as many people who *become* underburners. I call them *secondary* underburners. These lucky new members of the Jinxed-Metabolism Club don't get quite as fat as primary underburners. But their lives can still be a mess.

"What is happening to me?" asked Terri, age forty-five, beautiful but chubby for the first time in her life. "Everything I eat shows up on my hips. And I can't lose the weight anymore."

Terri, like most secondary underburners, did not change her pattern of diet and exercise. But her weight kept creeping upward, and she couldn't cut down on desserts anymore and watch the pounds slip off. By the time secondary underburners like Terri reach my office, they're always puzzled, frequently anxious, and occasionally hysterical.

In my most soothing tones, I told her to relax and join the "in" crowd. (I didn't say that "in" stands for "in hell.") "Nothing serious is happening to your body. You're forty-five, your metabolism is winding down from peak reproductive years, and you've become an underburner. It's not that you can't lose weight anymore, it's just that it's not as quick and easy—no more instant gratification."

For a stunner like Terri, that talk is hard to accept. But the sooner she faced facts, the more successful she was at recovering her former shape (or a decent approximation of it).

Unfortunately, most women can easily become underburners. All they have to do is stuff their existing fat cells beyond capacity at a critical time in their lives. By "critical," I mean hormonally active, and that means puberty, pregnancy, menopause, and any time they take a pill that seriously alters their metabolism. Since their metabolisms change often, and since they can produce new fat cells until age fifty-five (while men stop making new fat at forty), it should come as no surprise that they need only the slightest provocation to underburn. Men, on the other hand, not only resist weight gain during periods of overeating, but even when they gain don't put on amounts commensurate with the calories consumed.

If the secondary underburner is lucky, the state might just be temporary. But if aging is the only factor—as it was with Terri—then major adjustments are in order. Let's look at the events that can turn a normalweight into a permanent or temporary underburner.

Permanent Circumstances

Age and the Underburner

Shakespeare didn't say it but I will: Age doth make underburners of us all. Alas, alas, and alack.

A few years ago, I was summoned to a large midwestern city to help settle a labor dispute. A major airline was about to fire a forty-two-year-old female flight attendant who'd been there for twenty-two years. Her crime was having exceeded her hiring weight by a percentage the airline considered unacceptable.

Carol was five feet seven inches and weighed 156 pounds, which was twenty-one more than when she came aboard. During her tenure, she'd had two babies and a major operation. In younger days, she fought the battle of the bulge with strong diet pills, and, when the company doctor refused to give her more, diuretics. Often she flew with a dangerously low potassium level. (A dumb idea: excessive use of diuretics can lead to heart and blood-pressure problems.)

Finally, Carol could not tolerate diuretics either. She entered a starve-binge phase, until she didn't have the strength or elasticity to punish her body anymore. And now, twenty-one pounds heavier, she was about to lose her job. Apart from her weight, her record was impeccable.

My role in the arbitration was to convince the airline that Carol's weight gain was not the result of gluttony or sloth but a natural phenomenon of female aging. She'd starved herself down to an unnaturally low weight (for her) to get the job in the first place and had sacrificed much over the years to keep it down. Now, at forty-two and a senior attendant, she was tired of the battle.

I was a surprise witness, part of the union's quest not just to save this woman's job but to strike down the whole concept of low-weight standards. The battle was fevered, intense. The airline's biggest fear was that once those standards went, all hell would break loose. Female flight attendants would balloon: Picture them struggling to waddle down the narrow aisles, jogging passengers' arms and tipping the plane precariously. Picture tired businessmen, accustomed to years of svelte, perky stewardesses reaching up for blankets and bending over for drinks, now forced to avert their eyes from a parade of happy hippos. Why, business would invest in video teleconferencing; the airline industry would be ruined!

Said a thin, chain-smoking female attorney, "The very core and spirit of this airline is symbolized by its flight attendants."

Frankly, I'd be less concerned with the weights of their flight attendants than the hearts of their pilots and the eyesight of their flight mechanics. But what do I know? I don't even like to fly. The airline spent most of the arbitration trying to discredit me: Who was I to say that women tend to gain weight as they age? Who was I to say that there were such things as underburners and that underburners gain more easily?

The case was withdrawn, finally. Carol was reinstated to placate the union, and the weight standards remained firm. Recently, I heard a story about an older flight attendant for the same airline who'd admitted herself to a hospital for IVs to lose weight. She didn't want to be fired.

I don't know why the airlines are so worried. Most of the women they hire are thin normalweights, who will at worst become *normal* normalweights.

And why was the airline so hostile to my testimony? It's a physiological fact that metabolism slows about 20 percent between the ages of 30 and 90. The drop affects a woman's weight more than a man's, since a man can maintain normal weight on an average of 3,500 calories a day. So if he cuts his calories by 20 percent, he can still consume 2,800— which will go far in a culture of low-fat foods, abundant vegetables, and light beer.

Women, on the other hand, whose maintenance levels are at least 1,500 calories less per day, will find that a 20 percent drop knocks them down to about 1,650 calories. I don't lose too much sleep over normalweights, though. They can make up for that drop by increasing their exercise. Essentially, they have become mild underburners, but they lack the ability to make new fat cells, so their weight gain is limited. True underburners, on the other hand, have millions more fat cells to fill. (Even if they're at an age when their bodies have stopped making them.) They must increase their exercise *and* diet. And not just any diet. A diet for underburners.

What causes the slowdown of metabolisms? A decrease in thyroid function (which always accompanies aging) could do it, followed by a drop in the basal metabolic rate. This would be a reasonable explanation for women, because the usual symptoms of dry skin, thinning hair, and fatigue are also symptoms of decreased thyroid. Also, as a woman's reproductive cycle ends, she needs less internal energy for ovulation and pregnancy preparation of the uterus. Finally, there's an exchange between fat and muscle proportions in the body during aging, and the fat needs fewer calories to sustain itself.

The last point is probably most responsible for the slowing of the male metabolism. As a man ages, his muscle-making androgenic hormones decrease. And the fat that's left doesn't stimulate the resting metabolic rate as well as muscle does. Females already know that. Men who experience this metabolic shift should make an effort to build up their muscles. That doesn't mean pumping iron until your heart says, "Forget this!" (No one expects you to look like Rambo.) It means maintaining the muscles you have at near-peak levels. That's the best way for men to remain normalweights.

Nowhere in the female life-cycle (except pregnancy) are vitamins so essential to good health. A mature female underburner (either primary or secondary), under the stress of reproductive failure (menopause) and afraid to eat well because of weight gain, must take vitamins and minerals to feel her best.

Minerals are the most important: zinc for immunity; calcium for osteoporosis (a degenerative bone condition); and iodine for a faltering thyroid output. Increased amounts of the B vitamins, which are constantly flushed out by dieting, are also essential. Vitamins A, C, and E are antioxidants, which could be helpful in preventing metabolic changes that increase your risk of cancer.

This doesn't mean you should O.D. on vitamins. The daily doses below are both protective and safe:

A—10,000 IU
B—One high-potency tablet
C—500 mg
Calcium—1500 mg
Zinc—30 mg
Kelp (Iodine)—150 mg
E—400 IU

Males could use protection at this age, too. But they need less calcium (500 mg) and iodine (50 mg) and more vitamin C (1000 mg).

Temporary Circumstances

Premenstrual Underburners

Most women who read this book already understand the concept of premenstrual syndrome (PMS). But there's a lesser-known concept that's been around just as long: premenstrual underburning (PMU).

The week before menstruation, when estrogen and progesterone levels are highest, certain women have intense PMU—hunger, cravings, fluid retention, weight gain, and, if they're dieting, difficulty losing weight. True underburners experience PMU less, probably because they have more natural estrogen. (Their fat converts other hormones.) Estrogen is a buffer to progesterone, the hormone that's probably the villain in PMU. (Estrogen has been shown to decrease appetite, progesterone increases it.) The bottom line is that both normalweights and *dieting* underburners will gain weight from three days to two weeks before their periods.

While underburners constantly live with these feelings of craving, fatigue, and easy weight gain, normalweights don't know what to make of them. Welcome to the party, girls! How does it feel to be an underburner? If it's intolerable, the first line of treatment is a low-salt, low-carbohydrate diet (see my diet for underburners). If that doesn't help, try 300 mg of vitamin B6, which decreases fluid retention. Fluid retention slows down fat burning, which in turn inhibits weight loss.

If conservative methods fail, you might ask your gynecologist or internist to prescribe a diuretic called *spironolactone,* which masquerades as progesterone in the body. It fools the brain, modifies the cravings, and can even discourage fluid retention. It does not do windows.

Underburners and Smoking

If you're an underburner, the most effective way to remain in the closet is by smoking. In fact, cigarettes even give normalweights a calorie-burning boost. Too bad they'll kill you, slowly and painfully. Nicotine decreases your appetite better than a diet pill. It raises your metabolic rate better than thyroid. But it will destroy you more efficiently than both combined. In fact, if diet pills were even half as deadly as cigarettes, they'd have been off the market years ago.

The sad truth, however, is that normalweights who smoke over one pack of cigarettes a day can expect to gain ten pounds after giving them up. Underburners, even latent ones, can put on as much as thirty or forty pounds. Surprisingly, underburners are usually more willing to give up smoking than normalweight females, who are more narcissistic and find it hard to tolerate even a twelve-pound weight gain.

Since cigarettes are such a terrible habit, I have started a stop-smoking program in my office. With underburners that's asking for trouble, but better they stop under my care—when I can help them from gaining unreasonable amounts of weight—than on their own. Unfortunately, most people come in *after* they've gained the weight. And most think they're eating so much because they miss the "oral gratification."

Excuse me while I laugh. I've heard that silly oral gratification theory so many times that I'm tempted to say, "I smell a psychiatrist." But no more shrink-baiting. Needing something in their mouths is not the only reason people turn to food. If it were, they could chomp on carrots or chew pencils, like I do. (I don't recommend it—it makes your teeth crooked.) No, this is biology at work. You're hungry because your appetite rebounds (with a vengeance) and your metabolism drops. You have temporarily become an underburner.

My program lasts six weeks. I give smokers a mild appetite depressant and chemically increase their basal metabolic rate. Then I wean them off the medication, all the while teaching them how to eat and exercise to prevent a major weight gain. Needless to say, this works wonderfully with normalweights, whose bodies readjust after about six months. But it poses terrible problems for underburners, who have a higher set point and usually have to struggle even with the added help of cigarettes. The underburner must accept a major lifestyle change— giving up not only cigarettes, but a 300-calorie advantage.

Medication and Underburners

I can't help noticing that almost every serious drug for males makes them impotent, while most drugs for females make them fat. The pills that manufacture the most underburners are the major tranquilizers, the antidepressants, and the beta blockers.

I first noticed this phenomenon during my psychiatric residency, when many of my patients gained a lot of weight on antipsychotic drugs (Thorazine and Stelazine) and on antidepressants called tricyclics. The higher the dose, the more likely the weight gain; and the longer patients had to take them, the fatter they got. This wasn't the result of stress or increased appetite, and diets alone couldn't keep them from gaining.

Since women are the most depressed segment of the population, they're also the major users of antidepressants. And do they ever gain weight. During my residency, I used to feel terrible for these women. When they arrived, they were depressed with no explanation; when they began to take antidepressants, they got depressed about getting fat. Many were in midlife and had self-image problems to begin with. This was making them worse.

My understanding male colleagues said, "Forget the weight gain and concentrate on the depression." I didn't listen, and I put my patients on low-calorie diets. They lost almost nothing. Overeating had little to do with these women's weight gain: They had become underburners. Since I couldn't take them off their antidepressants, I decided to treat the underburning, and I gave them small doses of an active thyroid called Cytomel to speed up their metabolism. You know what? It worked. My patients lost weight.

The victory didn't last, but not because the drugs failed. At the next big staff meeting, one of the head doctors said, "Isn't it wonderful that Barbara's psychotherapy is helping her patients lose weight!" Er, ah, not exactly. I volunteered that psychiatry was getting a valuable assist from thyroid hormone. Needless to say, I didn't get the "Most Valuable Therapist of the Month" award. In fact, my prescribing practices were forcibly altered.

Now, fifteen years later, I can say I was right. Research has shown that antidepressants and mood-altering drugs do indeed decrease thyroid function, which I think is why they promote obesity. And more progressive psychiatrists have started to prescribe thyroid hormone for their depressed, heavy patients.

The best drug news I've heard in years is the development of a new line of antidepressants that not only discourages weight gain but has actually been tried as a *diet pill*. (See my section on diet pills in Chapter 15, "Helping the Underburner.")

Lately, I've heard nasty rumors about the beta blockers, drugs that treat (and treat very well) such disorders as high blood pressure, rapid heartbeat, and panic attacks. *Oh, no,* I thought, *not the beta blockers, too*. Alas, preliminary evidence suggests that beta blockers block the enzymes or hormones needed to break down the fat cell during dieting. The good news is that exercise and diuretics, which alter either the form or the receptivity of fat-cell membranes, might counteract the problem.

Antibiotics and nonsteroid antiinflammatory drugs (NSAIDs) don't directly affect fat, but they seem to hold body water, and that slows down the fat-burning process.

Hormonal Suppression and Replacement Therapy

Birth control pills are the most effective way of preventing conception. But many young women fumble with foams and messy diaphragms because they think the pill will make them put on weight. In the normalweight female, the pill does cause fluid retention; and early pills, with their high dose of estrogen, did make it about 10 percent easier to gain weight. Now, however, with estrogen and progesterone doses as low as possible, the pill's fat-making potential is minimal—for normal-weights.

Underburners, as usual, aren't so lucky.

How they make it easier for underburners to gain isn't clear, but it's probably that darn fluid retention and its effect on fat regulation. Estrogen in general makes it easier to convert food into fat. If you're an underburner and you want to go on the pill, be prepared to cut your calories back 10 percent. Increasing your exercise will help, too. I also suggest 300 mg of vitamin B6, which cuts down on water loading and seems to impede the fat-making process. A little.

Where the birth control pill causes problems for normalweights, too, is in weight *loss.* No question, it makes diets more of a hassle. Thin women on the pill often can't get as thin as they'd like to be, but I think they should count their blessings.

After a shaky start, estrogen replacement therapy (ERT) for menopausal women is making a comeback. In the 1960s, doctors prescribed a lot of it for women whose ovaries had stopped. Then they discovered that estrogen replacement caused cancers of the uterus, and the practice was sharply curtailed. A while later, researchers discovered that the cancer was due to cell stimulation of the uterine lining; if the estrogen were combined with its sister hormone, progesterone, the lining would slough off every month. This, indeed, is what happens naturally during child-bearing years. The new estrogen-progesterone pills reduce the risk of cancer significantly.

Why take it at all? There are good reasons. Estrogen helps protect the calcium in your bones from osteoporosis, which makes them brittle and crumbly. It also maintains the moisture in your skin and vagina, protects your muscle mass, and eliminates the side effects of menopause, among them hot flashes and depression. Estrogen makes women look better, and it helps them retain their feminine build.

Does it promote the storing of fat? Big question. Females finally get a break at 55, when they stop making fat cells. Does the hormone that keeps them vigorous also keep them heavy? Believe it or not (and good news is so rare when it comes to these drugs), it looks as if it doesn't. Research suggests that the plusses of ERT outweigh the negatives, and that weight gain doesn't seem to be a problem. The production of new fat cells is probably tied to fertility, and hormone manipulation in later life doesn't bring that back.

Underburners and the Third Shift

Have you ever noticed how many chubby people work on the third shift, the one from midnight to the time the rest of us get up? Many reasons spring to mind. Third-shift workers tend to have lower income levels, and statistics tell us that this group is the fattest. Perhaps they're ashamed of their appearance and prefer to work alone, at night, spending most of the day asleep. Maybe they're vampires—who knows?

What really interests me about the third-shift worker is his *circadian rhythm,* which relates to the body's internal time clock. Human beings are simply engineered to be awake during certain hours (during the day) and asleep at others. People who reverse that cycle interrupt their circadian rhythm and suffer metabolically. One way is by underburning.

If you work the third shift, you should limit yourself to two meals on workdays and no more than a 60-calorie snack between the hours of midnight and 7:00 A.M. I've also tried long early-morning walks as a means of circumventing distorted circadian rhythms, and the results have been excellent. Forty minutes four times a week is the rule of thumb.

The Masked Underburners

Secondary underburners should not be confused with masked underburners. These are the fat people who assure you they were thin most of their lives. All of a sudden, they say, they got very heavy. Just like that. The fickle finger of fate.

They used to puzzle us, the masked underburners, because we always assumed they were normalweights. It turns out that their thinness was a freak. Sometimes it was because they couldn't get enough food as kids, or else they had such limited tastes that they couldn't get fat. A few suffered from chronic infections like tonsillitis, which kept their weight in check. Some, especially women, were chubby during latency; grew out of their chubbiness because they got tall (five feet seven and over); kept thin through their teens (usually by starving); lived a swinging single lifestyle with an empty refrigerator; dieted strenuously to attract a husband; married; settled down; began to eat regularly; got pregnant and gained fifty pounds; lost twenty-five after delivery; and then started metabolically to behave like an underburner.

The masked underburner is often the tall or musclebound male. With age and a drop in androgenic hormones, his muscle mass decreases, his basal metabolic rate drops, and his natural tendencies resurface. This isn't muscle turning to fat; it's fat replacing muscle. Since fat requires less energy to maintain than muscle, the male underburner no longer has the advantage of an increased basal metabolic rate. Yet he continues to eat as he did in his youth.

Diabetes and Underburners

Adult-onset diabetes, the kind you get in midlife, can make you an underburner, too, but a different kind of underburner from the ones I've been talking about. Diabetics have a special kind of fat accumulation— the females are top-heavy. But the biggest difference is that diabetics don't create new fat cells; the ones they have just get very, very big. These cells are so big that insulin—the hormone that's supposed to regulate blood sugar—can't clamp onto them. So it can't store any sugar in them, and, as a result, the sugar levels in the blood stay high. That's what causes all the problems: strokes, kidney disease, heart disease, neurological disorders, and so on, not to mention obesity.

My theory, and it's just a hunch, is that the underburner's ability to create new fat cells could be his safety valve for regulating high blood sugar. The diabetic, on the other hand, just stuffs and stuffs the ones that are there.

The good news for adult-onset diabetics is that diet and exercise *work.* If you can shrink those colossal fat cells, the insulin can clip onto them and do its job. You get weight loss *and* a drop in blood sugar; and the drop, in turn, helps weight loss. That's because there's less insulin in the blood, and insulin blocks the burning of fat.

I used to think that underburners and diabetics had the same disease. Wrong. Diabetes has its own genetic program, its own agenda. Out of the one hundred overweight underburners I see every week, few are diabetics. The good news for underburners—the silver lining to all this —is that being fat doesn't seem to increase your risk of contracting diabetes.

Chapter 7

PREGNANCY AND THE UNDERBURNER

Feeding the Fetus, Not the Fat Cells

Pregnancy and lactation are the two times in a female underburner's life when she can naturally *burn.* Yet many emerge from this period much fatter. What goes wrong?

The mothers, I fear, are misinformed. And it's not hard to see why. The subject of diets for pregnancy is marked by strong emotions and a lot of irrational thinking. I remember a nasty letter from a nutritionist in response to the pregnancy chapter of my first book, *The Woman Doctor's Diet for Women.* I'd been especially careful with this section, enlisting the aid of my conservative gynecologist husband, as well as the chairman of obstetrics at a major hospital. The reason for caution is obvious: No one wants to write something that could even conceivably endanger the health of a woman and her fetus. So my book advised all pregnant, overweight women to eat a balanced 2,300 calorie diet, free of refined sugar and relatively low in fat and to take special vitamins.

In the nutritionist's letter was a newspaper article about a doctor being sued because a baby he'd delivered was born with microcephaly (an unnatural smallness of the head). The suit maintained that the defect had been caused by a diet the doctor had prescribed in the second trimester of pregnancy. The diet consisted of fruit, rice, and water. That's it. It was obviously absurd and bore *no resemblance* to a balanced 2,300-calorie regime for *overweight* women. And besides, microcephaly is a genetic accident; it would have nothing to do with what a woman eats in her second trimester.

So why would a nutritionist—someone who's supposed to be informed—even think of making comparisons? The roots of the controversy are in a radical change in obstetrical philosophy over the past twenty years. When I was having babies, doctors made us crazy about not gaining too much weight. Now they've reversed themselves. For more than a decade, they've advocated liberal weight gain, which is supposed to make for larger, more intelligent, and healthier babies. Their logic was inspired by studies of starving Appalachian women, who produced undersized babies.

Think a minute. Isn't it ridiculous to compare a starving woman to an underburner on a 2,300-calorie maintenance plan of protein, carbohydrates, fiber, and vitamins? You don't hurt your baby on that much nutrition. What concerned me was the effect this new, reactionary weight-gain philosophy would have on women who entered pregnancy already overweight, underburners who were suddenly being told to eat for two. I didn't think these women needed to gain thirty or forty pounds to have a healthy baby. In fact, food that makes them gain that much is often junk—empty calories.

A weight gain of more than twenty pounds on an already overweight woman will emerge after delivery as part of *her* body, and this new fat can create problems that last a lifetime. The 2,300-calorie diet was not for the purpose of weight loss; it was to help overweight women keep from gaining what they'd never be able to lose.

The letter stemmed from the nutritionist's failure to recognize and respect body differences. She wanted the same diet for everyone. But females entering pregnancy can have one of several different body types.

There are normalweights who gain twenty to thirty pounds and emerge after delivery five to ten pounds heavier than their prepregnancy weight. Those pounds are usually gone by the six-week checkup.

There are normalweights who enter pregnancy underweight, but nature sees them through. Food is converted right to fat, until the women have the proper blood volume and nutritional state to support a pregnancy. These are the models who talk about gaining forty to fifty pounds during pregnancy and look svelte by the time their kid is two months old. "By my six-week checkup I could almost model bathing suits again," they brag. "Except for a teensy-weensy tummy." Underburners hear that and want to shoot themselves. What the models don't tell you is that they were thirty pounds underweight to begin with.

These women are not mentally superior to underburners; their advantage is biological. The weight they gain in pregnancy is probably a different kind of weight, related to increased fat-cell filling for a temporary emergency state. Once it's over, the fat cells empty and the normal-weight returns to normal weight.

Now take the underburner, who enters pregnancy overweight and with a higher set point. This is a woman who can create new fat cells faster than a pigeon can void. If she eats more than the fetus needs, she might gain thirty to forty pounds during her pregnancy, at least fifteen of them by increasing her fat cell *number*. After she has the eight-pound baby and loses a lot of water, she's left with fifteen pounds of fat. She might shed five or six of them by decreasing the size of her fat cells, but she probably won't lose the rest. This is fat she'll carry with her into her next pregnancy, when the cycle will repeat itself.

It doesn't have to happen this way. If you're an underburner, you can have a normal, healthy baby and not have other hungry mouths to feed —by which I mean those brand-new fat cells. Fortunately, a lot of obstetricians are coming around. Some have begun to look closely at a woman's prepregnancy weight and build and are advising her to eat according to her individual needs.

It's a double shame when an underburner gains so much weight in pregnancy, because this is one of the two times in her life when she behaves like a normalweight. Pregnancy raises basal metabolic rate, and so an underburner doesn't have to undereat to maintain her weight. What pregnancy doesn't change, unfortunately, is the ability to make new fat cells. So when her obstetrician tells her to eat all she wants, the results can be disastrous. She'll follow orders, all right. Wouldn't you?

The other time an underburner acts like a normalweight is when she breast-feeds. Have you observed the girdle of fat a girl acquires at age thirteen or fourteen? That's the reserve fuel she needs to feed the child that nature is preparing her to bear. This fat must always be available for nursing babies, and it strongly resists breakdown (by diet and exercise). In the last trimester of pregnancy, however, as levels of prolactin (the milk-producing hormone) rise, the fat suddenly becomes accessible. To produce milk for a nursing baby, you require 700 to 800 calories of energy, and you get it from you-know-where.

A baby and a bonus.

The High-Calorie Pregnancy Maintenance Plan

Breakfast:

4 oz. orange juice or 1 serving fresh fruit
1 or 2 eggs (cooked any way) and 1 piece of dry toast *or*
1 cup cold unsugared cereal and skim milk

Beverages

Decaffeinated coffee, tea, nonfat milk, tomato juice, seltzer

10:30 A.M.

8 oz. skim milk
2 plain crackers *or* rice cakes
Pregnancy vitamins

Lunch:

1 sandwich (using two pieces of bread, not a roll)
The filling must be either beef, chicken, or turkey, *or* tuna (1 tablespoon mayonnaise allowed per can) *or* skimmed-milk and cottage cheese *or* low-fat regular cheese
lettuce and tomato (if desired)
ketchup or mustard
fresh fruit or Jell-O (1 serving for dessert)

3:30 P.M.

8 oz. skim milk
1 plain cracker *or* rice cake with 1 tablespoon peanut butter *or* 1 container lowfat yogurt

Supper

6 oz. lean meat, either beef, chicken, turkey (broiled or baked), or
    fish
all the salad you want with diet dressing or oil and vinegar
2 cups cooked vegetables, except corn or peas
½ cup brown rice
1 serving fresh fruit

Snack

1 complex carbohydrate or fruit, unbuttered popcorn, yogurt bar

Chapter 8

THE MIND OF THE UNDERBURNER

Putting Up the Best Defense

Underburners start out to be pretty average people, with the same hang-ups and minor personality problems that afflict everyone else. But at some point in their development, their personalities change, doubtless the result of their treatment at the hands of normalweights.

Every normalweight seems to have a strong opinion about under-burners, and chances are you're going to hear it. Sometimes you get it on the bus from a little kid who blurts out, "Mommy, why is that man so fat?" Sometimes you get it in a restaurant, from people who simply don't like to watch underburners eat. (As my own daughter once put it, "I just hate to see heavy people chow.") You get it from the salesperson who steers you with a sigh to a larger-size rack, from the friends and acquaintances who give you unsolicited advice about what to eat and wear. ("I saw the cutest dress on this large woman yesterday and it made her look so thin—I'll bet you'd love it!") You get it from noble souls who try to convince you to go with them to the gym every other day, certain that in no time you'd be as trim and fit as they are.

Normalweights think this kind of bludgeoning is not only morally justifiable but in some respects their *duty*—if all else fails, they reason, they can shame the underburner into losing weight. The upshot is that it's only human for underburners to develop a number of defense mechanisms to protect themselves from a hostile environment. Here are a few of the more common:

The Intimidated Fats

The Intimidated Fats decide that if you can't beat 'em, join 'em. They tend to be kind, well-meaning people who don't like to be conspicuous. Normalweights will like them, they feel, if they don't make waves, don't eat in public, and bake cookies for all the bake sales. They think normalweights are disciplined, knowledgeable about nutrition, and justifiably outspoken; "They're doing it for our own good," is how they describe their persecution. Privately, they consider themselves weak, inferior, undisciplined, and generally abnormal; and they tend not to seek out their own kind.

The Fat Cats

Fat Cats follow the *"I'll show them"* philosophy. They don't love being fat, but they've achieved some personal success in spite of their appearance. Sometimes they're successful by actually making fun of their weight. ("The shape I'm in," says Rodney Dangerfield, "you could donate my body to science fiction.") But more often they just decide they have to be that much better than the competition. Fat Cats are usually self-employed professionals or freelance humanitarians. They are rarely in large industries, banks, or other prestigious institutions, where normalweights have decided that no one beyond a size 36W waistline or a size 12 dress will be in any condition to climb the corporate ladder.

I guess I consider myself a Fat Cat. I'm reasonably content to maintain the status quo, except for certain self-imposed times of dieting zeal, often related to promoting my books. (You can't go on television hawking a weight-loss book if you look like a failed customer—although I've tried.) I've had my share of harassment, not only from normalweights who can't tolerate a Fat Cat dispensing diet information but from frustrated former fatties who keep thin by starving themselves or exercising to within an inch of their lives, and who can't see why I won't do that, too. Former fats don't turn their hostility on the normalweight world; they reserve it for their still-chubby comrades—and themselves.

Fat Cats can hide behind their success, too. Often they want to change but are too stubborn to try. That *"I'll show them"* attitude occasionally breaks down into spiteful-child behavior in the face of criticism. But they're rarely as hostile as those in the next category:

The Militant Fats

This group was long overdue. Biologically, fat makes both men and women more placid and maternal, so any rebellion tends to be internal. But the rise of the feminist movement in the late sixties and the seventies helped them find their voice, and you can find large numbers of them fighting the good fight on a number of fronts.

This is still the smallest segment of the overweight community, but what they lack in numbers they make up for in pounds and brains. Their style tends to be paranoid, and they dress to emphasize their weight instead of hide it. Don't get me wrong. I *like* the militant fats. If they tend to be hostile (even to me on occasion, because in their view, diet books just reinforce the normalweight status quo), their hostility is at least directed at the outside world, *where it belongs.*

Because of their weight, however, their credibility suffers. No one really believes they like being fat. But credible or not, they are the ones who will push for reforms, uncover job discrimination, and dramatize the plight of the intimidated majority. More power to them.

Discrimination against fat people won't stop until underburners begin to tell normalweights to mind their own business. They must shape (not *re*shape) a new identity for themselves, an identity built on pride in who they are and not elaborate defenses for what they're not. They must bring financial and legal pressure to bear against their oppressors, instead of trying to starve themselves into conformity. Underburners should be free to decide if they want to lose weight and *why* they want to lose weight. They mustn't allow doctors to intimidate them, newspapers to deride them, or society to exclude them.

There's no question, however, that fat in the young is a social curse; it would be naive to think we can change that (although it is the duty of our schools to try). It's also a fact that as you age, moderate to severe obesity impairs the quality of life—it makes you less mobile and more prone to complicated ailments. If you want to live longer, you'd be far better off a little thinner; but that choice should be *yours* to make, and you shouldn't make it solely in response to a hostile and uncomprehending world.

Chapter 9

THE UNDERBURNER'S DIET

Art Buchwald once called *diet* "the verb meaning 'to die.'" What an optimist. I'd amend the definition to "the verb meaning 'to die slowly and painfully and go to a hell of raw vegetables, puffed rice cakes, and diet soda.'"

In the seventies the word *diet*—which once referred simply to a person's daily food regime—came to mean "weight-loss diet" exclusively, but lately it's gotten mixed up with terms like "healthy diet," "balanced diet," and "sensible diet." Let's get one thing straight: we're talking about a *weight-loss* diet here, and it's not balanced, healthy, or sensible to reduce your calories to semistarvation levels for the purpose of burning fat. It's a physical and mental ordeal, made necessary by nature's mistake in allowing some humans to accumulate too many fat cells.

My job is to make of this unpleasant and unnatural situation a diet that promotes reasonable weight loss, that can be tolerated for as long as you need to lose weight, and won't endanger your health. It's a dirty job, but someone's gotta do it right.

A Diet Should Promote Reasonable Weight Loss

So what is "reasonable" weight loss, anyway? As far as dieters are concerned, weight never comes off fast enough. And the underburner loses more slowly than most. In fact, underburners sometimes lose so slowly that I tell them to write down the number of pounds they deserve to lose and then divide by two—the result will be closer to what they *will* lose.

Since there's little consensus on what constitutes "reasonable" weight loss, let's define "rapid" and "slow" loss. Low-calorie diets (under 1,000 calories) promote what I call rapid weight loss. In females, this still means only seven to ten pounds the first two weeks and two to two-and-a-half after that. (In males, that figure can almost be doubled.) In the first three days of a diet—the part that makes everyone hysterically happy—a whopping 70 percent of the weight loss is water, five percent is protein, and a mere 25 percent is fat.

Diets over 1,000 calories promote slower weight loss and have been touted as safer, more effective, and lasting. I believe the saying is, "The slower you lose, the slower you gain back the weight." But those are normalweight rules again. Normal folks think a diet longer than ten days is long. When they go back to eating regularly after, say, seven days of grapefruit and canned salmon, they quickly replace their water weight. So they conclude that it's better to lose weight more slowly, which to them means (horrors!) a full two weeks of dieting. (Even if they gain their weight right back, they still feel thin for two weeks instead of one.)

Underburners, who often must diet for two months, do better when they lose faster. Otherwise, after weeks and weeks of infinitesimal losses, they're ready to eat the scale.

Thanks to free enterprise, any quack can concoct a weight-loss plan. Pick a diet, any diet. You can have a high-protein/low-carbohydrate diet—meat and salad and no bread—but that's hopelessly out of style. How about a trendy high-carbohydrate/low-protein diet, which might offer whole-wheat spaghetti with marinara sauce, whole-wheat bagels with sugarless apple butter, and lots of oatmeal? Or you can go the Chinese starvation route and purify your body both physically *and* spiritually (and, along with other anorexics, end up in the hospital for emergency refeeding). For a change of pace, you can opt for any one of a thousand diets that revolve around a low-calorie fruit, vegetable, seed, or grain.

I don't object to some of these diets on medical grounds; they're okay, just different ways of skinning the cat. If you must diet, it's fun to be on the "in" plan now and then, and this is one time when underburners can join their normalweight friends. Alas, after ten days of cutting calories, normalweights emerge slim and exuberant, while underburners continue to munch their nuts or seeds, drink twelve glasses of water a day, and choke down those bananas and seaweed. The goalpost can seem a million miles away.

The funky, silly "in" diets are for normalweights. Underburners need a diet with staying power, a diet that can adapt to their changing needs.

What Is a Good Diet?

1. A diet that gives you choices, so you can live with it.
2. A diet that uses the metabolic effects of food and food combinations.
3. A diet that takes into account what kind of loser you are.
4. A diet that is a simple thing, but good.

A Diet That Gives You Choices

Have you noticed the popularity of some of those expensive, hideous-tasting, calorie-controlled frozen dinners? And have you noticed that no one seems to lose weight very effectively on them? I guess that where diets are concerned, people lose their inventiveness; they want someone to dictate exact portions of specific foods. I think that's one reason so many diets fail—because so many dieters are helpless without their frozen dinners or superdetailed menus. They never learn the *principles* of successful weight loss.

Back in the 1970s, when I devised my original Core Diet, my husband kept bugging me to spell out a daily menu, such as: *Tuesday, dinner, 4 oz. poached scallops, 5 spears steamed asparagus, 1 6-inch wedge watermelon,* and so on. I resisted. That's fine for normalweights, but can you imagine an underburner—whose diet might span two seasons—worrying about asparagus in December or watermelon in March?

I gave people credit for having more imagination. When I said they could eat four ounces of lean meat or fish, I figured they'd think of chicken, beef, liver, swordfish, halibut, turkey, and so on, without my having to choose one for them. I still think so, and maybe that's not such a commercial idea. But dammit, I've seen too many people break their diets when they've been short one measly ingredient on a strict plan—and they didn't know what to substitute!

You can successfully follow the Underburner's Diet in all seasons, moods, periods of financial bust (or boom), and on most foreign vacations. And once you learn the principles, you can comfortably devise higher-calorie variations on it for the rest of your life.

A Diet That Uses the Metabolic Effects of Food

The *basal metabolic rate* is the amount of energy a person expends when he or she is at rest. And that's the heart of it, boys and girls—how much your body tends to burn when you're talking on the phone, watching TV, or just existing. There are three major components of the basal metabolic rate, as you can see in the pie below. (Sorry to use a carbofat to represent the BMR, but in a discussion of the underburner's metabolism, maybe it's appropriate.)

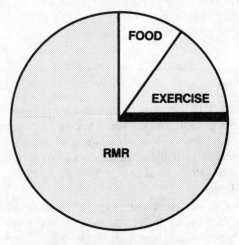

Basal Metabolic Rate

You can see that food and exercise account for only about 25 percent of your BMR. A much more significant factor is the *resting metabolic rate* (RMR), which is the bugger that, in all likelihood, determines whether you're fat or thin. The RMR controls a person's natural (or set-point) weight, and it appears to be genetically programmed.

A fourth and negligible factor in calorie-burning—the black area on the pie—is the body's thermostatic control system, which helps you adjust to changes in temperature. Certain fat cells (known as *brown fat)* actually have nature's equivalent of thermometers in them. It's too bad the process doesn't use up more calories, since underburners do a lot of shivering.

So—for the time being, at least—we only have about 25 percent of your BMR to play with. We'll have to make do.

I once saw an ad that boasted, "You burn more calories eating and digesting a pickle than the pickle contains. So pickles actually make you lose weight." That's balderdash, frankly, but it's a neat idea—that you can use certain foods to stoke the metabolic furnace. All foods have what's called a *specific dynamic action* (SDA), which is the amount of energy the body uses to break them down. Since anything you eat must be digested, it follows that all foods raise your basal metabolic rate. So all foods are useful on a diet, right?

Alas, no. But some get your machine working harder than others. Not pickles, which *are* low in calories but are also mostly water. More useful, I've found, is protein.

Protein

Proteins are the body's building blocks; you need them for muscle and connective tissue growth. When you have to cut calories, they have other advantages. They do not stimulate your body's insulin production, and that means your blood sugar doesn't drop and you don't feel as hungry later on. Proteins also take a while to digest, so they make you feel fuller longer.

In my first book, I advised dieters to eat about seven ounces of protein a day. That's a lot by today's standards, and some self-styled experts have lately been clucking about the perils of a "high-protein diet." But it's still the right idea. Humans require at least one to one-and-a-half grams of protein for every kilogram of body weight, and the early stages of a diet can drain off a lot of your stores. So seven or eight ounces of animal or fish protein seems very prudent to me for the first few weeks. Eventually, the body learns to "spare" protein—which means it stops raiding your stores for additional energy. That means you can gradually decrease your protein intake in weeks three and four.

Back to specific dynamic action: Protein requires a lot of energy to burn, and it can raise your basal metabolic rate by as much as 9 percent. So underburners get a bonus—and they get mighty few.

Does anything else use up as much energy? Fat does, but it supplies nine calories per gram of energy burned—twice that of protein, so you end up losing nothing. Fat is also one of the reasons that protein gets bad press: so much meat is married to it that you ingest a lot more calories than you think. Another minus: protein doesn't supply much fiber, and you need that to keep your digestive tract in sound working order.

I now insist that my diets contain *scrupulously lean* protein, even if it has to be poached or boiled; and I incorporate fiber (in the form of bran or pectin) into all meal plans. Fish is especially low in fat, but it also takes less work to digest. For women—and especially women who don't exercise much—animal protein promotes more efficient weight loss.

Carbohydrates

Recent studies revealed that while protein and fat raise the BMR of fat women, there's no comparable rise with carbohydrates. The researchers were surprised. I wasn't. I hate to say "I told you so," but I suggested as much in my first book. For the female underburner, complex carbohydrates are like water in your gas tank.

Complex carbohydrates—bread, potatoes, starchy vegetables, pasta, and rice—are currently enjoying great popularity on today's diet scene. It's easy to see why: they're low in fat and high in health-food chi-chi. But in the dieting underburner, they stimulate appetite, block the burning of fat, and don't even raise the basal metabolic rate. They won't hurt you, but they'll throw your diet into an endless stall.

Several years ago, one of my chubby friends ignored my advice and tried the complex-carbohydrate, fat-free approach at a Pritikin clinic.

Fifty pounds overweight, she lost fifteen of them rapidly, but afterward she found that even by cutting down her complex-carbohydrate allowance, she couldn't shed another. She finally resorted to a raw fruit and vegetable diet to continue losing weight. In all fairness, however, she noted that the men in the program seemed to lose weight well even on large amounts of complex carbohydrates.

Then there was the Optifast crisis. Optifast is an excellent brand of liquid protein used in a diet called the "Protein-Sparing Modified Fast." This is a *very* low calorie diet (under 500 calories a day) made popular a few years ago by Drs. Blackburn at Harvard and Vertes and Genuth at Cleveland Clinic. PSMF uses small amounts of protein, even smaller amounts of carbohydrates, and vitamin and mineral supplements. It's not a casual diet; in other words it strives for rapid weight loss in the very obese. Optifast is the liquid version. It has 80 calories per serving and contains 14 grams of protein, 6 grams of carbohydrate, and less than one gram of fat. You're supposed to drink five packets of the stuff and take a lot of vitamins. That's all. Fun! Fun!

Then, when carbohydrates came into fashion, someone decided to increase the carbohydrate content to 20 grams. The protein remained the same, and the calorie-count rose to 160. Five packets now supplied 800 calories per day. Some men continued to lose weight briskly, but underburning females stopped losing weight. This continued, even when the calories were reduced as low as 480 per day. My underburning women stopped losing weight as efficiently. My underburning patients on the diet—women who were *starving* themselves for a dramatic loss—came in some days with no significant change in their weight.

I'm no fool. I went back to the regular Optifast. And I've been nervous about carbohydrates ever since: complex carbohydrates (starch), which often increase my patients' appetites and slow their weight loss; and simple carbohydrates (sugar), which are maddeningly addictive. At the risk of sounding melodramatic: *Beware.*

Fat

It's too bad fat is so terrible—it adds richness and creaminess to food, and it helps you feel more satisfied. As I noted above, it also has a whopping 9 calories per gram, which is twice that of carbos and protein. There's worse news yet: scientists now believe that fat is incorporated into *your* fat more easily than other types of food. Fat increases the viscosity (the stickiness) of blood, and sticky blood clumps together and attaches to the walls of blood vessels. This causes more clumping, interferes with blood flow, and impairs cell breathing. That's why high-fat diets can increase your risk of a stroke or heart attack.

If your blood isn't genetically equipped with efficient cholesterol scavengers, a fatlike cholesterol can deposit dangerous plaques on the insides of vessels. One patient of mine, a relatively young man with no health problems or family history of heart disease, died suddenly after a massive heart attack. He'd just eaten a very high fat meal (steak, baked potato with sour cream, salad with roquefort dressing, bread with butter, and apple pie à la mode) and followed it up with sex with his second wife. The coroner said the high-fat meal had clogged up his arteries. I said it was sex with his second wife. The point is, the *combination* is potentially lethal.

Decreasing fat in your diet can do more than protect your heart. High-fat diets have been implicated in certain cancers, particularly of the bowel and breast. Probably what happens is that breakdown products of fat accumulate in the bowel and set up a sort of toxic-waste dump that disturbs normal cells. (Fiber, which has a lot to do with how well you move your bowels, might offer some protection here.) In the breast, the mechanism of action is not as clear, although fat does help in the production of postmenopausal estrogen, which is a high risk factor in cancer. Fat intake in females might also have something to do with the manufacture of *prostaglandins,* a pain-causing hormone that contributes to menstrual cramps and arthritis pain.

A Diet That Takes Into Account What Kind of Loser You Are

A good diet for the underburner must be low in calories but not absurdly low—just under 1,000 calories for females and 1,500 for males is sufficient. The Underburner's Diet, the Mix and Match Diet, the old faithful Core Diet, and the emergency Restart Diet work well.

How do you know what kind of a diet is right for you? If you're a fast loser, you can get thin on any old diet. If you're a medium loser, an underburner's diet will give you a terrific push out of the starting gate, whereupon you too can shift to a more conventional weight-loss plan.

Though it's rare after forty, you are a *Fast Loser* if you:
    could "eat like a horse" when you were younger.
    have no menstrual problems, excessive bleeding, or hot flashes.
    are not taking drugs, especially antidepressants, NSAIDs,
        or estrogen.
    are "active" and do an hour of aerobic exercise a day.
    are a normalweight male.

You are a *Medium Loser* if you:
    are not more than thirty pounds overweight.
    have always had to be careful about what you eat.
    enjoy exercise.
    have not been on a diet in the past year.
    are taking no medication that would put on weight.
    are a male underburner.
    are a female underburner under age twenty-five.

You are a *Slow Loser* if you:
    are more than thirty pounds overweight.
    have just regained weight from your last diet.
    stabilized for a while but suddenly can't stop putting on weight.
    have a severe problem with fluid retention.
    work the third shift, midnight to eight A.M.
    can't exercise because of infirmity.
    take medication that enhances weight gain.
    have had major surgery lately.
    have just given up smoking.

A Diet That is a Simple Thing, but Good

In spite of my morbid cracks at the beginning of this section, I really don't believe you have to curl up and die when you diet. But I don't believe in sumptuous diet books either—you spend too much time planning your meals and thinking about food.

You can use spices to achieve flavors that you miss when counting calories. Tomato sauce, parmesan cheese, and oregano evoke the taste of Italy—so what if they pep up a chicken breast instead of a plate of pasta? Cumin and chilies are the taste of Mexico, curry powders conjure up the Taj Mahal, and fresh herbs—especially tarragon and basil—are like Paris in springtime. Well, not really, but in dieting a little fantasy goes a long way. So does a little succulence. A *drop* of oil can be a treat if everything else isn't dripping in fat. Ditto for a pinch of sugar, although watch yourself on that one—you don't want to trigger any cravings. These are your condiments. If you learn to use them sparingly, you just might find a little bit of heaven in this low-flame, underburning hell.

On the Underburner's Diet, you will know what every piece of food that goes into your mouth is there for. Not how many calories it is, since a calorie of protein doesn't work the same way as a calorie of fat. You'll know more important things: how your body converts it into energy; what nutrients it supplies; how it will fill you up; how it will make you feel.

We're going to take the sorcery out of dieting.

Before we march, let's review some basic strategies.:

- A diet should give you meals that make you feel full. Not enraptured or transported, you understand, but comfortable, satisfied. They should not leave you ruminating about more food.
- A diet should fill you up without too many calories. Water is the cheapest filler, so drink at least four glasses a day. This will also wash a lot of waste products out of your system.
- Fiber is a good filler, too. You can have your bran plain or you can mix it into something like meatballs. Sorry, you cannot have it in a muffin. Whenever possible, you should try to eat low-calorie fibers like pectin or guar, which probably interfere with fat absorption in the small intestine. And speaking of waste in your system, fiber will also give you bulkier, more regular stools, which you'll appreciate.
- Fluid, fructose, and fiber *before* a meal makes it less likely you'll gorge yourself during one. Fresh fruit supplies all of these, and it's essential.
- A diet must satisfy your carbohydrate receptors just a little, without going above your critical carbohydrate level and triggering a binge. Cooked vegetables make an ideal low-calorie carbo. You can also, if you're desperate, eat a plain breadstick afterwards. That's a *plain* breadstick if you're desperate.
- Protein will help get your basal metabolic rate up, which will

help you burn calories more efficiently. Make sure, though,
that it's not attached to fat, or it will gum up your engine.

- Sugar, refined as sucrose, will also slow your fatburning system. Avoid table sugar especially, and watch out for starches
  that act like sugars in some cooked vegetables (potatoes and
  carrots, in particular).
- A diet should be accompanied by what I call the *40 Times
  Four,* which means a 40-minute walk four times a week.

The Underburner's Diet

Breakfast

1 piece of fruit, whole, *not* juice
Two egg whites, scrambled, and chives
Decaffeinated coffee (with diet sugar, if necessary)
or
1 egg (boiled, poached).
1/2 a thin slice of whole-wheat toast
or
Liquid protein, not to exceed 110 calories, and with at least 9
grams of protein. Or make your own protein drink with 1 egg, 4
oz. skim milk, 2 oz. orange or pineapple juice (or 1/2 banana),
and one tablespoon bran.

Lunch

A salad with diet dressing or
Steamed mixed vegetables

Small serving of lean meat or fish or
1/2 cup cottage cheese (low-fat, if available)

1 whole-wheat, nonfat, unsalted breadstick if you're still hungry.

Dinner

4 oz. clear soup (bouillon, consommé), tomato juice, or small
salad

1 Pectin or Guar pill

½ fruit (apple, orange, melon, or grapefruit)

Lean meat or fish

Tossed salad with diet dressing or steamed vegetables

1 whole-wheat nonfat, unsalted breadstick if you're still hungry

Beverages:

4 glasses of water
Unlimited decaffeinated coffee, tea, diet soda
Tomato juice when you need a pick-me-up

Vitamins:

You must take the following supplements daily with all low-calorie diets in this section:
Vitamin A (4,000 I.U.); B–C complex (1 tablet); calcium (1,000
milligrams) with vitamin D (250 milligrams); vitamin E (400
I.U.); potassium (300 milligrams).
1 multivitamin

Before we go through this regimen food by food, point by point, you probably want to know what I mean by the ambiguous phrase "lean meat or fish," and how much you can eat of it.

Women can have three to four ounces per meal. Men can have four to six. That's how it goes.

By lean meat, I mean:

Beef: Flank steak, tenderloin, ground beef less than 17 percent fat (round or sirloin), round steak (London broil). **It must be trimmed of all visible fat.** Beef may be broiled, baked in a broiling dish (so the fat drips to the bottom), grilled, or dry sautéed. The latter means you should use a spray fat if you're going to use anything.

Chicken: White and dark meat, no skin, no wings. You can eat the heart, liver, and giblets (trimmed of fat).

Turkey: White and dark meat, no wings. You can cook it with the skin but peel it off before you eat.

Cornish hen and squab: You can eat what you want. The skin is thinner on these birds and there's not much fat by the time you finish cooking them.

Poultry can be broiled, baked, grilled, or poached in bouillon or white wine.

Pork: Tenderloin. Baked.

Veal: Chop, scallopine, or ground with less than 17 percent fat. Broiled or grilled.

Lamb: Medallions (center of loin chop). Broiled.

Calves' and beef liver: Broiled or baked.

Frankfurters: Less than 17 percent fat. Boiled or grilled.

Deli: Roast beef, trimmed of all visible fat. Turkey breast, no skin. Smoked turkey breast (if salt is no problem).

Seafood: Clams, mussels, oysters, scallops, lobster, crab.

Fish: Salmon, bluefish, swordfish. These are slightly fatty, and must be broiled dry or with herbs and lemon.

Halibut, cod, scrod, and sole may be broiled with mustard-yogurt sauce or baked with onions and tomatoes (canned or fresh).

Canned: Water-packed tuna, salmon, sardines and mackerel (both drained of oil and washed).

Breakfast

Whole fruit: Once again, fresh fruit supplies fructose, fiber, and filler. Fruit juice, on the other hand, offers little fiber and filler and a lot of concentrated sugar.

Scrambled egg whites: They're pure protein and will raise your BMR. The protein source is important here to start the body running. The last thing you want is a heavy-carbohydrate breakfast (what the majority of Americans consume), which will stimulate your appetite.

Decaffeinated coffee: This is always preferable to caffeinated, because caffeine raises your insulin level and blocks the burning of fat. And you don't need to be any edgier. Use caffeine only when you need a pickup, at natural low times like midafternoon.

A whole egg: It gives you more cholesterol than just the whites, but that's no problem for women with low cholesterol and no family history of heart disease. All men plus women with high cholesterol should probably stick with whites whenever possible. But don't worry too much. Weight loss alone lowers your cholesterol about 15 percent.

Whole-wheat toast: Unlike white bread, this has fiber, so it fills you up better. If you're going to eat carbohydrates on a diet, make sure they're mixed with fiber.

Grapefruit: Fructose or fruit sugar satisfies your sweet tooth without triggering your appetite the way table sugar does. Grapefruits in particular are low in calories and go far toward filling you up. People also tolerate them well—they usually don't upset your stomach or cause a lot of allergic reactions. For the most part, they're readily available and inexpensive.

Liquid protein drinks: These are good for underburners as long as they're low in carbohydrates. Unfortunately, the sweeter drinks stimulate your appetite and encourage you to drink more than you need; if they're high in carbos, they can block the burning of fat.

Optifast and some other good liquid proteins are *barely* palatable. That's not so bad—at least no one will want to O.D. on them. My homemade version isn't terrific-tasting, either (that's why I added the fruit) but it does include bran. I also add bran to some of the commercial liquid proteins, if they're low in fiber.

The case against breakfast. What about skipping breakfast? Some severe underburners swear that protein in the morning makes them nauseous and that carbohydrates both exhaust them and stimulate their appetites. If that's how they feel, there's no reason they should have to eat breakfast.

Underburners are usually not hungry in the morning. They wake up in a mild *ketosis,* a metabolic state in which fat is burned and the appetite suppressed. You're in ketosis when you feel bouncy and your breath gets *very* bad. It's nice not to be hungry for a change, even with bad breath. So why eat? Remember, you really can operate on your existing fat, with maybe a smidgen of carbohydrate to protect your muscle mass and a hot low-calorie liquid to stimulate the gastro-colic reflex and get the bowels moving.

A lot of nutritionists will tell you that breakfast gives you an energy boost, and in some cases they're right. But most Americans eat carbohydrates and fat in the morning, which can make the underburner feel more sluggish. For the underburner in the morning, movement fuels the metabolic pump much better than food.

Lunch

Lunch must not be skipped.

Ever.

It should be as close to midday as possible, or, barring that, as far from supper. Too many fat high-school kids wait until they get home to start eating, so they might have a 1,000-calorie snack at four and a 1,000-calorie dinner at six, before they're finished digesting the 1,000-calorie snack. For the underburner, this kind of eating is a one-way ticket to obesity.

Underburners often eat less than they need during the day and save up all their calories for one big meal. That's one reason they don't lose weight—their systems work better with smaller, evenly spaced feedings. Let's say you eat 200 calories at breakfast, 350 at lunch, and 500 at dinner. That makes 1000. You'll lose more weight than someone who just eats 900 calories for dinner and nothing the rest of the day, even though that person has consumed fewer calories overall. Don't overload your system.

Salad with diet dressing or steamed mixed vegetables: Both offer (all together now) filler and fiber. And they're low in carbohydrates, and so they won't stimulate your appetite.

Lean meat, fish, or cottage cheese: This is protein to raise your BMR and fill you up. Cottage cheese is a little risky since it has modest amounts of fat and carbohydrates. But it's convenient—often the only acceptable protein available—and it makes for a change.

Whole-wheat, nonfat, unsalted breadstick: If you're still hungry, this should satisfy your complex-carbohydrate receptors without stimulating your appetite. Remember, if the complex carbo is dull enough and includes a lot of fiber, it won't trigger overeating.

Dinner

This is the heaviest meal for the Underburner. Ideally, it should be the lightest meal. (It's the end of the day, and unless you're going to disco all night you probably won't be moving around as much now.) But we do not live in an ideal society and dieting is not an ideal situation. By following certain rules, you can make dinner less dangerous.

One low-calorie filler: Have clear soup, tomato juice, or salad as a first course. Drink water. Just get something filling and safe into your stomach so you don't chow down the first thing you see. (Bread, for example, if you're in a restaurant.)

1 Pectin or Guar pill: Fiber. Need I say more?

1/2 fruit: This will also help curb your appetite, especially if you have to wait a while before the meal comes, as in a restaurant.

Lean meat, fish, or chicken: This is very important in the evening, when your basal metabolic rate tends to drop.

Breadstick: This is only if you're still very hungry. Again, it will satisfy your carbohydrate receptors.

Food for Thought

- The difference between salad and steamed vegetables is that steaming ruptures the starch molecule and makes for more satisfying food than just the bulk and fiber of salad. The trick is to steam *lightly* to retain the filling quality of fiber and still unlock that starch.

- The practice of eating between meals is a bad habit for the underburner. Don't do it. Meals are when you eat; between them is when you work, play, exercise, run errands, read, and think.

    Nibbling is the underburner's worst enemy. Even if you nibble on low-calorie food when you diet, when you stop dieting you'll nibble on high-calorie food. If you make one behavioral change as a result of this diet, make this one.

- You can successfully stay on this diet in any restaurant, but you have to do one thing. **Ask how it's cooked.** Then tell the waiter how you *want* it cooked, with apologies to Chef Jean-Pierre. You want it steamed, boiled, or broiled *without butter.*

In restaurants, if you want to have fun, you can substitute for fruit in the first course. Raw oysters and clams are marvelous, but nix the sugary cocktail sauce. (Try lemon and horseradish instead.) Ditto for shrimp and crabmeat cocktails. A whole artichoke takes forever to eat, and if you pass up the butter (make that *"when* you pass up the butter"), you'll get fewer calories than you'd think. Sample hearts of palm or asparagus, with the vinaigrette on the side. (You're allowed a teaspoon of it.) Plain consommé and tomato juice are fine. If you must have a cocktail, have a glass of wine or a Bloody Mary. You do not need to try the paté. The snails in garlic butter will not be offended if you don't have a taste.

You may eat that slice of kiwi on top of your friend's pie.

- Dinner parties will take all your willpower. For some reason, most people would rather commit hara-kiri than phone a host or hostess and ask about the menu. So be it. If you think the spread will be a lu-lu, however, and you don't trust yourself, eat your dinner beforehand and spend the party talking, sipping club soda, and smiling like a fiend.
- Since this regime can be a long-term commitment, you can feel free to adjust for the seasons. On this diet, an apple and a slice of watermelon are more or less the same, except that an apple tastes better under a tree with red, yellow, and orange leaves and watermelon tastes better on a beach. Don't deprive yourself of *all* aesthetic satisfactions.

The Mix And Match Diet

Many people tell me it's easier to diet when they don't have any choices. "Spell it out," they say. Or they claim they'd rather eat nothing than just a teensy bit of food. This all-or-nothing philosophy is what made the liquid version of the Protein-Sparing Modified Fast diet so popular.

To remind you, the PSMF is a very low calorie diet (below 500 calories) made up of a high-quality liquid protein and designed for very obese people. On rare occasions, in patients of rare girth, I go the whole, er, hog and give them five packets of Optifast a day. I'm convinced, however, that this diet's value is limited. It engenders the kind of social isolation that makes for severe mental stress, and you can't undertake it without a battery of psychologists, physical therapists, and physicians in the wings.

But I do love the diet I call Mix and Match, which uses two Optifast meals (usually breakfast and lunch) and one normal meal. It's a good diet for underburners because of its low-fat, high-protein, and low-carbohydrate combination.

Breakfast

1 orange
Liquid protein supplement (mixed with water, diet soda, club
    soda, or skim milk)
Decaffeinated coffee or tea.

Lunch

Liquid protein supplement (mixed as above)
1 small salad with lemon juice and vinegar
Decaffeinated coffee or tea

Dinner

4 oz. meat or fish
2 cups salad with 2 tablespoons diet dressing
1 cup cooked vegetables (if you want corn or peas, reduce to ½
    cup)

The meat-and-vegetables meal can be eaten for lunch or dinner. Actually, you tend to lose faster if you eat it for lunch.

Don't forget the vitamins, the same regimen as in the Underburner's Diet.

This diet assures you of a two- to three-pound weight loss weekly. Given the severe restrictions, that might not sound like much. But on a regular three-meal-a-day diet you'd be losing only one-half to one pound a week.

This type of diet is especially helpful for the older dieter who eats alone, doesn't want to slave over meals, and needs only a few highly digestible calories and an adequate amount of protein. He or she should, in addition, sprinkle a tablespoon of unprocessed bran on the midday salad.

If you are over sixty, don't even *think* about trying this diet without a complete physical examination first.

You can stay on the Mix and Match Diet until you've lost all your weight. But because your intake has been so low, the first month of your maintenance period should include one liquid-protein meal a day. You don't want to shock your system too much with all that solid food.

The Restart Diet

I created the Restart Diet for returning patients who'd lost a lot of weight and then, alas, gained it back. I noticed they had a much more difficult time losing weight the second time around—it was as if their fat cells didn't want to be broken down again. Somehow the little demons were together.

So I gave them a jolt. I cut calories down drastically and flooded the system with liquid. The water loss seemed to stun the body momentarily, and the sudden drop in calories got the fat-burning mechanisms going. Often in two weeks most of the regained weight was lost and the body was now equipped with more receptive fat cells.

Research has since proved that fat cells do get more resistant with each repeated episode of dieting. They learn to hold out at lower gear, knowing—in a greasy, primitive sort of way—that they're eventually going to be fed. So if you must start all over, RESTART. If you can't get going after a major or minor diet infraction, RESTART. If you're in a carbofat-eating frenzy, RESTART.

Day 1	Nothing but liquids and diet Jello-O, divided into meals if you want. You can have decaffeinated coffee, tea, diet soda, water, diet gelatin, bouillon, spinach broth, clam juice, tomato aspic, tomato and V-8 juice, and low-fat milk.
Day 2 *Add*	9 oz. of lean meat or fowl or 12 oz. of fish or seafood, divided into two meals
Day 3 *Add*	2 large salads with oil-free dressing and raw vegetables
Day 4 *Add*	*Breakfast:* 1 orange; 1 egg or egg white, boiled; 1 rye cracker
Day 5 *Add*	2 cups green or white steamed vegetables
Day 6 *Add*	2 melba toasts
Day 7 *Add*	2 more fruits

Stay at this level for one week.

The only problem with this diet is there can be a rebound on the third day, which functions like a binge after a fast. So at this point be sure to start exercising.

Chapter 10

THE UNDERBURNER'S DIET FOR MEN

Men can lose weight on almost any diet. I used to put them on whatever fad diet struck my fancy—and would hold their interest—and they almost always did well. I've had a change of thinking lately. Sure, a male will lose weight a lot more easily than a female; but men tend to have more serious health problems than women, so their diet should encompass more than simple weight loss. It should promote overall good health.

Men die about seven years sooner than women. They have more diseases of the heart and intestinal tract, and more complications of high blood pressure. A medical journal recently suggested that the male is less biologically able to protect himself from noxious influences in the environment—among them pollution, chemical additives, and cigarette smoke. Female hormones, the theory goes, can weaken these influences. We know for a fact that estrogen protects against heart disease in the menstruating female.

There is also an "all or nothing" aspect of men's health: when they are well, they are superb, but when they're sick, *oh boy*. Statistics show that while women between the ages of 45 and 65 visit their doctors more, men suffer from more illnesses requiring hospital stays. My mother has a female friend with a "heart condition," and we are always expecting her to drop dead. In spite of that condition, she has outlived three husbands, all succumbing in a relatively short period of time from bowel cancer, lung cancer, and a heart attack respectively. Once doctors learned to keep women from dying in childbirth, the female emerged as the biologically stronger of the sexes.

I think nutrition can play a protective role in male health, not just by eliminating obesity, but by improving total fitness. Many wives used to brag about their "meat and potatoes" husbands, and it wasn't considered manly to eat low-fat cottage cheese and salads. Now we realize that diet is a major vehicle for toxins, and some toxins cause cancer. So the male diet in this book will be geared for detoxification as well as weight loss.

Weight loss for the male underburner can be achieved at a much higher calorie level. A man is able to reach the metabolic state of ketosis faster than a woman, and to sustain it much longer. This state decreases appetite and, as long as lost minerals are replaced, increases energy. Males in ketosis are also high emotionally, and are zealous about their dieting commitment. It sometimes alarms their female companions, who complain to me, "He's so dedicated to this diet, it's nauseating."

The most important metabolic difference between the male and female underburner is that the male can tolerate complex carbohydrates better than the woman; and it's beginning to look as if they should be eating more of them. By *tolerate,* I mean that men can eat carbohydrates, lose weight at a reasonable speed, and not run the risk of increasing their hunger.

A weight loss diet alone will substantially lower a man's risk of illness. This diet is low in saturated fat and high in fiber, so it should reduce the risk of cardiovascular disease and bowel cancer. Fiber is like the scavenger sponge of the intestinal tract—bulking, binding, breaking up, and absorbing all waste material. If it didn't, those waste products would be converted into potential carcinogens.

I think dieting and nondieting males should be on high-potency vitamin supplements; if they're going through a rough patch, they should up their dosage. Vitamins A, E, and C might afford some protection against cancer. Men, with their illogically raging hormones, are always under stress of some sort, and need constant buffering. They can get it from the vitamin Bs.

Breakfast

One fresh fruit

One serving cooked or uncooked whole-grain cereal with one tablespoon unprocessed bran and one cup skim milk

Alternates:

Two boiled eggs (to be eaten only three times per week, and only if blood cholesterol is less than 220 mg.%)

One slice unbuttered whole-wheat toast or small whole-wheat pita
or

One whole-wheat or pumpernickel bagel with low-fat cottage cheese or diet margarine.

One glass of water with 5,000 IU vitamin A, 400 IU vitamin E, and 500 mg vitamin C, and 10 mg zinc.

Decaffeinated coffee or regular tea, if desired with milk and artificial sugar

Fruits can include orange, banana, grapefruit, melon. If fresh fruits are not available, substitute one heaping tablespoon of raisins.

Dry cereals can include Bran Flakes, Corn Flakes, all non-sugared rice cereals, Grapenuts, Shredded Wheat, Product 19, Special K, and Chex.

Midmorning: Small glass of nonfat milk or tomato juice with one multivitamin and one B supplement.

Lunch

One sandwich on dry whole-wheat or rye bread with lettuce and tomato, if available. Possible fillings include lean white meat chicken or turkey, roast beef, fish, or seafood

Small salad, optional, no dressing.

One fresh fruit, optional
or

Large chef salad, with one meat and one cheese, oil and vinegar dressing (limit oil to one tablespoon)
or

Large spinach salad (no bacon), with one tablespoon of prepared dressing.

or
Fresh fruit salad with low-fat cottage cheese
Two breadsticks or rye crisp crackers can accompany the salads.
Diet or club soda
One glass of water
Decaffeinated coffee or tea

Midafternoon Snack: Two whole-wheat crackers, with small glass
 of skim milk or tomato juice.

Dinner

Five ounces (cooked weight) of any lean meat, fish, poultry, or
 seafood.
One large serving of cooked vegetable.

Mixed vegetable salad with onions and tomatoes.
Diet dressing or one tablespoon oil and vinegar
100 calorie starch, if desired: 1 small potato, or ½ cup white or
 brown rice.
One fresh fruit.
One pectin pill.
One glass of water.
Decaffeinated coffee, regular tea, low-fat milk.

Beef intake at dinner should be limited to three times per week and
can include tenderloin, lean hamburger (less than 17 percent fat), and
flank steak.
 One dinner weekly should include a fatty fish like salmon, tuna, or
swordfish.
 Chicken can be cooked with the skin, but the skin should be removed
before eating.
 Carrots, broccoli, and/or spinach should appear at least once. Eat
only fresh corn, and if you want more than one ear, subtract one ounce
of meat. No peas.

 Evening snack (at least one hour before bedtime):
 One 4-oz. glass of skim milk *or*
 2 cups plain popcorn *or*
 one frozen diet bar (yogurt, fruit, frozen confection) *or*

diet Jell-O with fresh fruit.
One combined fish oil pill

On the male underburner diet, I have not been as careful about what you eat first or last. There's no problem putting fruit first if your hunger is intense.

Free foods. Raw vegetables and plain diet gelatin. If diet soda does not give you personality problems or seizures, I have no objection to your drinking it; just don't go above one quart daily. Water intake should be six to eight glasses daily. Of course, this amount varies with outside temperature and activity. I have never known any normal male to voluntarily dehydrate himself.

Alcohol is important to some men. Whether it's a social drink with a client, or a relaxation drink at home, it can be an integral part of people's lifestyle. The good news is that a *moderate* amount of alcohol might protect you against heart disease; the bad news is that alcohol supplies 7 calories per gram, more than carbohydrates. But if you want that drink, and it will keep you on your diet, take it from your meat. You can have two drinks a day *(tops),* but you must eat two ounces less meat.

Exercise is also important to protect your muscle mass. It's not a good idea to work out with weights at the beginning of a diet. Aerobics like walking or running more specifically target fat, and you'll have time to see how your body is handling its losses. There will be plenty of time to develop muscle after the diet.

Chapter 11

AND A-WEIGH WE GO

Getting Around the Obstacles

In addition to a good diet, there are many vital components of an underburner's weight-loss plan. These include:

1. An accurate scale
2. A monitor
3. Realistic expectations
4. Time
5. A health care provider who will not sabotage you
6. Peer support
7. An understanding of what's happening to your body
8. A maintenance phase

An Accurate Scale

I can't tell you the difficulties I've had with bathroom scales. They're a joke. Step on one gingerly and it will respect your need for a low, inaccurate weight. Wiggle off those pounds in seconds!

It would be terrific if every underburner had a doctor's balance scale. That's quite an investment—over $300—but no more expensive than any other piece of major health equipment. And at least it won't lie to you, josh you, pamper you, and change its mind daily.

If you don't have a good scale, slight differences in weight don't register, and it's hard to monitor slow losses. You're also at the mercy of different scales, among them your doctor's (one visit a year) and your health club's (two times a week). These scales have their own margin of error—after all, they weren't designed to weigh titanium.

If you can't buy a doctor's scale, at least be consistent and get weighed at the same time of day, in the same type of clothing. I used to wonder why so many of my patients wore superthin clothes in the middle of the winter.

Underburners get weighed too much anyway. They don't lose quickly enough, especially after the first week, and stepping on the scale every day inevitably depresses them.

The Monitor

Since it's common practice for a long-term dieter to drift away from a diet between weigh-ins, it's wise to find someone who will keep checking up on you—a monitor. Most diet programs have official monitoring systems. They range from biweekly encounters with a nurse and a scale (as in my office) to daily confession sessions (as in some of the more born-again diet clinics). To each his own monitor, but a monitor there must be. I used to let my husband do it, but too many snide remarks cost him his job. The monitor must be impartial.

Unfortunately, I know a few diet doctors who give patients a diet and a six-week supply of diet pills and say, "So long. Godspeed." Six weeks later the patients come back with their empty pill bottle and their weight depressingly the same. They've had no anchor all that time, and they've drifted out to sea.

Realistic Expectations

There's nothing like unrealistic expectations to screw up a diet. The ads and testimonials you read feature men and women who've lost a lot of weight quickly; no company's going to emblazon their brochures with an underburner struggling to lose a pound or so a week.

Most normalweight women can lose seven to ten pounds in the first two weeks of a diet and two pounds a week after that. There will be weeks they'll lose more, but they can't count on it. Men lose almost twice as much, eating 800 more calories. Female underburners lose about a pound a week, but if they exercise they can sometimes knock that up a notch. After all, there's more of them to lose.

The safest plan, however, is not to expect too much. I tell my underburners that if the weight fell off them, they wouldn't be in my office in the first place.

Weight loss varies according to what's going on in your life. Stress alone can gum it up, and so can medications and surgery.

The older you get and the more you've dieted, the more resistant your fat cells become to being broken down. "Not again," you can almost hear them whine. It's more difficult after a while to overcome that inertia and make your body begin to burn fat. In some cases, it can take six weeks. It's almost as if your fat cells are stonewalling you, convinced they can wait out the siege. That's the bad news. The good news is that once the fat does start to burn, it should go as efficiently as ever—*provided* you gradually increase your aerobic exercise.

In fact, as the diet nears its conclusion, exercise becomes almost as important as diet, although neither alone will do the job.

Time

I've alluded to the normalweight's idea of a diet, the Ten-Day Blitz or Two-Week Crash. Unfortunately, the underburner has been lulled into believing this is his time frame, too. No such luck. Even the most disciplined underburner has to diet for at least a month to get permanent and meaningful results.

Say an underburner loses ten pounds in two weeks. Only about four of them are fat; the rest is water and protein, and the body will immediately correct those losses when normal eating is resumed. For normalweights with only five or six pounds to lose (they always say they need to drop ten, but they'll live happily with five), the diet is over. For the underburner, who has fifteen or more pounds to lose, it's just beginning.

Most people can diet for two weeks. Fewer can diet for two months. One in a thousand (maybe) can diet for two years. Only 5 percent of the dieting population ever loses as much as forty pounds. *Time defeats diets.* That's why it's so crucial for the underburner to keep his weight gain within reasonable limits—so his diets have a prayer of succeeding.

A Health-Care Provider Who Will Not Sabotage You

There are two types of health-care providers—the trained and the programmed. The former are physicians and nutritionists; the latter are the
folks who run the diet centers, men and women who've been handed a
credo (sometimes good, sometimes not so good), a lot of buzzwords,
and a chart.

Normalweights can go to programmed providers because their dieting experience is usually short, and, as a result, free of complications.
But every so often I hear a weird story. Like the time one spotted a
patient of mine drinking diet soda and said, "You shouldn't be drinking
that! It's got too much salt!" Talk about stealing candy from a baby.
How many other luxuries do underburners have?

You can't really blame the programmed health-care providers—at
least, you can't blame them any more than you would a good Samaritan
who stops at the scene of a car accident and inadvertently moves a
victim with a broken neck. He doesn't know any better! Programmed
health professionals are just hired guns, and they're only as informed as
their parent organization wants them to be.

The trained health-care professional is another matter.

Take the nutritionist. Please. I recall an old saying about why surgeons operate so often: "If your only tool is a hammer, then everything
looks like a nail." You could say the same about today's nutritionists—
they think every ill can be treated with diet. And what a diet: a calorie
is a calorie is a calorie, no matter who's doing the eating. Young, old,
fat, thin: what's the difference? A diet, they say, should be 15 percent
protein, 30 percent fat, and 55 percent carbohydrates. Period. And
they're so damned *correct* all the time, so positive in an area where we
know almost nothing for sure. Nutritionists are useful in feeding the
homeless, the kidney-impaired, the dying cancer patients; but when it
comes to underburners, where flexibility and an open mind are more
important than micro- and macronutrients, they're a lost cause.

Even worse saboteurs of a good diet program are doctors, who really
ought to know better. But for ignorance, rigidity, and lack of creativity,
they are peerless. They're more dangerous than nutritionists because
their impact on lives is much greater. Here's one medical mismanage-
ment I recently witnessed.

Into my office came Max, a sixty-two-year-old male; eighty pounds
overweight and in terrible shape. His doctor hadn't sent him to lose

weight; a close friend had. His condition, however, was so borderline (cholesterol: high; uric acid: high; blood sugar: high; blood pressure: high; breathing: labored) that I promptly called his primary-care physician to let him know about all these problems. Why he wouldn't know, I had no idea—Max had just had his yearly physical.

Not only did the physician resent my calling him, but he didn't believe my tests, and he suggested Max return to him so he could corroborate the results. Max, no dummy, said no thanks. He was happy to let me have a shot.

Today, after a year of treatment, I have a thin (he lost all 80 pounds), vigorous (he walks four miles a day with energy), healthy (his blood tests are normal), sexy (he chases his wife around the bedroom), and happy patient. And what did Max's internist say when I returned him after the diet? Did he call and apologize for his brusqueness? Did he inquire how the miracle was accomplished? (Counseling, a simple diet, and gradual exercise is what I'd have told him.) No. He didn't say anything.

There are other stories: Doctors who tell overweight patients they shouldn't be dieting; doctors who put obese patients on high-calorie diets after surgery; doctors who prescribe high-calorie foods to treat stomach ailments; doctors who give medications that make people gain weight but refuse to let them know (or worse yet, lie, as in, "Well, Mrs. Chubb, I can't imagine why you're gaining weight. The Elavil you're taking for sleep couldn't possibly be doing it!")

I don't want this book to degenerate into a harangue about medical men (and some thin women). There are physicians who begin with the best intentions and *then* get turned off. The problem is *their* unrealistic expectations. When a doctor sees a fat person walk into the office, he has rescue fantasies. ("I will rescue this person from his own indulgence. I will show him the way.") The doctor knows that if this patient would just lose weight, he'd look better, feel better, live better, and love and be loved better.

Success seems inevitable (it's all so logical), and failure remote. Then treatment begins, and what looked simple becomes a little more complex; what looked complex becomes impossible. Physicians have big egos. When they can't accomplish what they set out to accomplish, they get anxious and angry; finally, to protect their egos, they detach themselves altogether. They grow disinterested in treatment.

In their defense, there's no other specialty (except psychiatry) in which physicians see such self-destructive behavior go on for so long. And psychiatrists *choose* psychiatry; general physicians have something more predictable in mind.

In order to change doctors' attitudes, they must first be taught that obesity is a chronic metabolic problem that cannot be solved simply by trying to change a patient's behavior. Sure, if these people could give up fattening foods entirely and turn themselves into aerobic athletes, they'd have no need of drugs or counseling or complicated diets. But most of them aren't up to that—they're only human. So, unfortunately, are their physicians.

Peer Support

The support of your peers is an essential part of a successful diet. This means the hostess who makes sure there is food you can eat at her lavish dinner party; the husband or boyfriend who takes you to a fish house instead of a pizza parlor; the child who says no to a box of cookies for fear you'll be tempted. Family, friends, husband, lovers—all can make your nasty ordeal more bearable. And all can sabotage you.

There's active sabotage and passive sabotage. Active means offering you candy or goodies during a diet; making you feel guilty if you don't eat something that's been "lovingly" prepared for you; or attacking you for your unprecedented rigidity. ("You've been a real bitch since you started that diet!") Active sabotage can topple the less determined dieter, but at least you can see your saboteur and make a conscious decision to fight.

Passive sabotage is far worse because its methods are indirect. You're left to struggle with yourself, and that's the hardest battle of all. The passive saboteur is the friend or spouse who says *nothing* while you diet and diet and wait in vain for encouragement and approval. It's the mother who keeps forgetting to buy diet food, the brother who eats what she does buy, the doctor who fails to notice that you're twenty pounds less than you were last year.

The younger you are, the more you're at the mercy of saboteurs. As you age, you learn to spot them and, more than that, to confront them with their treachery. One box of candy tossed before their eyes into the garbage will deter all further lethal purchases; a private stash of diet food will make pilfering less likely. Remember, passive saboteurs are jealous and afraid. They're jealous you'll get thin and give them competition; and they're afraid that you'll change for the better, that you'll develop some confidence and think a little more about yourself.

Those are clear indications that you ought to prove them right.

Chapter 12

UNDERSTANDING WHAT'S HAPPENING TO YOUR BODY

There's a lot more to weight loss than the calories in a cucumber or the vitamins in an orange. Dieting is really about your body's (and mind's) reaction to disturbances in normal eating patterns. If you're alert, a diet can teach you what was wrong (or right) with those patterns in the first place. If you're not, you might never learn why certain foods affect your body in certain ways. Like by coating it with flab.

When you lose weight, major physical and metabolic changes take place. There's a drop in blood pressure, blood sugar, blood lipids (fats), and body water. Most of the time these changes are good. But sometimes they lead to nasty side effects, especially on long-term diets.

Mood swings, for instance. Dieters hurtle from misery *(I'll never be able to lose these thirty pounds)*, to anger *(I'm going to eat what I damn well please)*, to impatience *(It seems like I've been dieting forever—this* after one week), to fear *(Yipes, I have three parties next week)*, to boredom *(If I eat another carrot, I'm going to have orange hair)*. It's no surprise that you can burn out on a diet in as little as two weeks.

Patterns of weight loss vary. You can lose fast for a while; slow down as your body adjusts to fluid loss; reach a plateau; gain, lose, gain, lose (the seesaw effect); and regain in a hurry. These patterns are intensified by the stress, temptations, and demands of the workaday world.

Who said diets are simple? I've never seen a long one without some unexpected difficulties, anything from serious hormone problems to a range of symptoms that include fatigue, constipation, excessive gas, depression, difficulty concentrating, sleep disturbances, slow pulse rate, postural hypotension (feeling light-headed when going from a sitting to a standing position), hives, hair loss, cold intolerance, irregular menstrual cycles, and impotence. Just to mention the more common ones. You want exotic? In underburners, weight-loss diets can also precipitate gallbladder attacks (in females) and gouty arthritis attacks (in males).

On the other hand, these symptoms might have nothing to do with your diet. One of my patients had periods of intense disorientation, during which she had no idea where she was. She blamed the diet, of course, but she actually had a rare seizure disorder. Everything from fevers to hemorrhoids get attributed to weight loss, and it takes a trained health-care provider to follow up thoroughly on the complaints.

I approve of commercial diet groups that help normalweights lose the odd ten or twenty pounds. But I feel that dieting and maintenance for the underburner is a serious, long-term commitment, which sometimes requires vigorous medical intervention.

What Underburners Can Expect to Happen As They Diet

Hunger and Cravings

Naturally, when you cut down on your intake by 1,000 calories or more, you're giving up a lot of food, and you're going to be hungry. When you stop and think, it's a tribute to man's sensitive biology that even with a few million overstuffed fat cells—which could keep him alive for many months—he can still feel those pangs.

When you're hungry, though, you don't feel much like paying tribute, because hunger is *painful*. It is, after all, what makes babies cry the way they do. You can't ignore it; the best nonmedical trick I can suggest is that you learn to get high on it. With every rhythmical sensation of hunger, just think: "There goes another fat cell." Above all, don't *fear* your hunger. Those wailing fat cells feed you well.

Even if you can convince yourself that you're not hungry, a peculiar longing will come over you for a certain type of food—a craving. Cravings are something that underburners live with all the time, but it's only since normalweights have begun complaining about them (in connection with premenstrual syndrome) that they've received any serious attention.

The point to remember is that they're *inescapable* when you're in a calorie-restricted situation. In underburners, they're especially strong during high-protein–low-carbohydrate diets. If you give in to the cravings and eat sugar or carbofats, you'll become even hungrier. But if you opt for a high-carbohydrate diet, you probably won't lose weight. (And, oddly enough, you'll crave protein.) It's a no-win situation, which is why I like to mix food types at all meals.

Cravings are also annoying during the maintenance phase of a diet, when you start to add more food to your regular regimen. They're how your body promotes a fast refilling of your fat cells. Premenstrual cravings, on the other hand, are probably the body's biological trick to prepare semistarved females for pregnancy; underburners don't get them as severely unless they're dieting, because their fat cells are already quite full.

Cravings decrease in ketosis, the metabolic fat-burning state, and with moderate to heavy exercise—more than thirty minutes a day.

Energy and Fatigue

We have been brainwashed into thinking of food as energy. If that's the premise, the logical explanation for lack of energy on a diet is lack of food. But this is a normalweight conclusion. Normalweights *need* food energy—they burn 1,100 calories a day merely by breathing. But only part of that goes for energy; the rest is wasted as heat, or, more poetically, "futile cycles." Underburners use fewer calories and store what they don't need as fat.

Underburners, I'm convinced, get tired while they're *storing,* not burning fat. (If you want to get technical about it, I think they're exhausting their enzyme-transfer systems to untie free fatty acids from glycerol in the fat cell, so there isn't too much lipoprotein lipase left for energy.) The point is that they usually feel more energetic when they're dieting and burning. In ketosis, they're positively exuberant.

The time the dieting underburner feels really depleted is during the big initial water drop, when he or she loses a lot of *potassium*. Potassium is a mineral that's vital for muscle strength; you know you're low if you feel weak, disoriented, have muscle cramps, or get light-headed when you change positions.

Most high-potassium foods are too high in calories for a diet—you'd need twenty-five inches of banana to replace just one day's loss. Low-calorie sources, like spinach and cauliflower, aren't very practical or available. (Can you imagine an executive on a diet producing a head of cauliflower during a meeting? "Excuse me while I take my potassium break.")

I give my patients potassium supplements. The problem is that they're not commercially available in adequate doses without a prescription. (Potassium can be dangerous for people with sensitive stomachs or advanced kidney disease.) If patients object to supplements (they taste godawful), I suggest a tasty, low-calorie, and easy-to-make potassium broth. Simmer together four cups of chicken bouillon with a pound of spinach. Drain the spinach into a bowl and pour the liquid you've pressed out back into the broth. The spinach you can save for some recipe or other; it's the broth that's the magical pick-me-up. Twenty minutes later, you'll feel great.

If you go to a physician and say, "I'm losing potassium," he might give you a blood test. Chances are, it will be negative. For some reason, a dieter's low-potassium state doesn't show up in the blood. (The potassium loss is probably from the entire body, including muscle and fat.)

Plain fluid depletion, which happens on low-carbohydrate diets, can also trigger fatigue and headaches. You're simply dehydrated. Four glasses of water daily in addition to other fluids should replace the lost volume.

Another possible reason for fatigue in dieting is hypoglycemia—low blood sugar—which can cause you to feel weak, faint, and dizzy. Energy is supplied by sugar (glucose); the problem here is that it takes a little longer for your body to get sugar from your fat than from food. It *will* get it, but there just isn't an instantaneous response to the demand. That's what makes you light-headed.

You can get this "reactive" hypoglycemia after intense exercise, an extended fast, a few alcoholic drinks, or whenever there's a lot of insulin in your blood looking for sugar molecules that haven't been liberated from their fat cells yet. The best way to avoid it is not to exercise too strenuously, eschew fasting and boozing, and ingest something low in calories like tomato juice or skim milk—both of which have enough nutrients to satisfy your insulin but won't wreck your diet.

Sleep Disturbances

Most people sleep well on diets, happily dreaming of fat cells burning in the night. Every now and then, however, someone has a lot of trouble falling asleep and staying asleep. If you're taking diet pills, the culprit is obvious—those little monsters can leave you nervous and agitated long after your house has gone dark and your spouse has begun to snore. Most of the time, the cause is ketosis itself, the fat-burning state that makes people hyperalert. Ketosis also sensitizes you to caffeine and other stimulants, which you'd be otherwise able to handle. (When you're in ketosis, alcohol acts as a stimulant instead of a depressant, so nix the nightcap.)

If you have a sleep disorder, take nothing that could act as a stimulant after four in the afternoon. You should also try to raise the levels in your brain of a chemical called serotonin, which plays a crucial role in sleep. Tryptophan, an amino acid available in health food stores, will raise your serotonin levels. Better yet, a four-ounce glass of warm skim milk at bedtime is rich in tryptophan and really will help you sleep. (You can also have an ounce of lean meat.) If all else fails, try two tablets of acetaminophen (the ingredient in Tylenol and other aspirin alternatives), which will buffer your nervous system.

What you shouldn't take on a diet is a sleeping pill. It will give you a hell of a hangover.

Vitamin and Mineral Deficiencies

Some patients tell me that they never got sick until they started to diet. "But your body is getting fed by your fat," I'd protest. There's one thing I missed, however: Fat is food without most nutrients, vitamins, or minerals.

It is *imperative* that you take supplemental vitamins and minerals on a weight-loss diet. Here are the reasons:

1. Dieting underburners will not take in enough food to meet vitamin and mineral needs.
2. Studies have suggested that certain immune mechanisms re-

side in fat. When you burn off the fat, you lower your immunity. Vitamins help the immune systems.
3. Vitamins enhance certain enzyme systems that break down fat.
4. Certain vitamins (B_6) promote natural diuresis (water loss).
5. Constant water loss washes out the B vitamins (not to mention potassium and sodium).
6. Certain minerals (like iodine) can increase thyroid function.
7. Low-fat intake lowers the absorption of fat-soluble vitamins (A, D, E, and K).
8. Dieting is a stressful time. Depressing, too, even if you're successful. That makes you more vulnerable to illness. Vitamins can mitigate stress and improve your mood.

Begin with a good multivitamin. Add a high-grade B and C supplement plus extra calcium, iodine, zinc, and potassium.

Digestion

Many symptoms can plague an intestinal tract; a sound weight-loss diet can actually relieve them. For the older underburner, a *hiatal hernia* is probably the most miserable ill. It's caused by a hole in your diaphragm that permits the esophagus—the long tube that connects the mouth to the stomach—to pass through. When the hole gets wider with wear and tear (usually caused by fat and increased abdominal pressure), the top of the stomach can slip up through the diaphragm and sit in the chest. This causes all kinds of symptoms, ranging from heartburn, chest pain (often mimicking heart-attack pain), high back pain, light-headedness, and irregular heartbeats. It's not a lethal situation in itself, but it's no one's idea of a picnic.

Weight loss, I'm happy to report, will let you put away your antacids and stomach pills. Not only will it decrease the pressure on the stomach and shrink its distension, it will also increase the muscle tone of the esophagus, so that acid in the stomach won't splash into the chest. This will reduce (and in some cases stop altogether) the hiatal hernia symptoms.

The symptoms of *irritable bowel syndrome* (formerly spastic colon) include constipation and diarrhea (they alternate), gas, and abdominal pain. IBS happens when stress, diet habits, or an inherited defect cause an interruption of the bowel's natural rhythms, making the feces move too fast or too slow. It might be related to food allergies, too. The best treatment is a low-fat, high-fiber diet that eliminates the most common allergens (fat, wheat, corn, and milk).

This is a good place to talk about fiber, the savior of IBS sufferers. Fiber is the undigested residue of food that reaches the last digesting part of the small intestine. Along the way it actually absorbs fat and cholesterol and decreases the time it takes to pass a normal bowel movement. There are three groups of fiber: vegetable, bran, and chemically purified. The latter, such as pectin, cellulose, and guar gum, is the most effective in absorbing fat.

For bowel regularity, bran is a good fiber to include in a diet (although it doesn't absorb much fat). I suggest two tablespoons of unprocessed bran a day, followed by eight ounces of water. (This bran is like sawdust—you won't get it down without liquid.) In this way, you not only ensure an adequate amount of fiber but also virtually eliminate the constipation that comes with a decrease in water, calories, grains, and bulk.

If you don't like your bran straight, make a Bran Betty by adding two tablespoons to a half-cup of unsweetened applesauce and all the artificial sweetener and cinnamon you want. You can also add it to a package of diet gelatin. Two tablespoons mixed into a cup of steamed mushrooms makes a good stuffing. For something heartier, try bran spinach meatballs: four ounces of lean ground beef, two tablespoons of bran, a half cup of spinach, and any herbs or seasonings you like.

Many other conditions have been mistaken for irritable bowel syndrome. One of the most common is *lactose intolerance.* Lactose is milk sugar, which requires an enzyme called lactase to break it down in the large intestine. Some people don't have any lactase after a certain age, so the lactose is left to intestinal bacteria to break down. That means *lots* of gas. Many can tolerate a small amount of milk, but exceeding a certain level provokes unpleasant symptoms. The best treatment is *pre*treatment—you can buy lactase at drugstores, add it to milk, and let it sit and react for a day. Presto: predigested milk. You can also take lactase in pill form.

Certain diet foods cause trouble. The sorbital sugar molecule (in sugarless gum and candy) is too large to be digested in the small intestine, so it goes to the large intestine, where bacteria gets to work and triggers much internal distress (external distress, too, if there are family and friends present). Beans, lettuce, the whole cabbage family, and the skins of certain fruits also break down into gas-producing substances. On a diet, it's relatively simple to eliminate those foods one at a time and see if symptoms persist.

Allergies

In the last few years, allergy treatment centers have advanced the theory that fat is related to food allergies. This is, in a word, bunk. If one of these centers runs a questionable test, claims that you're allergic to wheat, sugar, or dairy products and advises you to eliminate them from your diet, you're going to lose weight. But it won't be because you gave up foods you were allergic to. It's because you gave up fattening foods.

Allergies to food can cause a lot of symptoms besides the traditional hives, swelling, itchiness, and runny nose. They probably cause fatigue, headaches, joint pain, and dizziness to name a few. But not fat. Often I'll take patients off a sensitive food if they have some of the above, but it won't make them lose weight any faster.

Probably the food allergy that's received the most press is mold. This is one allergy for which allergy shots have been moderately successful. (Most of the time, allergists are just jabbing in the dark.) A mold-free diet helps, too. That means you can't eat aged meats, pickles, cheese, wine, smoked substances, peanuts, vinegar, or leftovers.

Don't confuse an allergy with a sensitivity; foods containing methyl xanthene (caffeine and chocolate, among them) act as toxins on certain end organs in the nervous system causing pain, headaches, irritability, and sleeplessness. Caffeine is now, thanks to a good variety of decaffeinated coffees and diet sodas, simple to bounce from your regimen. As for chocolate, it never should have been there in the first place.

You don't need any fancy testing to confirm and control a food allergy. But you must be methodical and keep good records. Cut out one class of food at a time for about two weeks and see what happens. Start with wheat and continue through corn, milk, and foods with mold. You might be allergic to more than one substance, but as one of my colleagues put it, "Allergy is a rain barrel. A lot of water drips into it to fill it up, but until the last drop makes it overflow, you won't have symptoms." So if you can lower the level in the barrel and keep the last drop from falling, most allergy symptoms will go away.

Menstruation

Weight-loss dieting can do anything to your periods. It can make them regular or irregular, heavier or lighter, painful or less painful. It can stop them altogether. It can make you infertile.

Diet and exercise that seriously deplete the young female of body fat (as in anorexia, a very low calorie diet, or heavy sports participation) will halt periods. But there is something more interesting. When underburners go below their set-point weight—but not necessarily to skeletal levels—their periods get scanty and further apart. There's reason to believe that women also stop ovulating. Understand, these women aren't starving themselves. They're just operating at levels that nature considers inappropriate for reproduction. When carbohydrate is added back into the diet and an acceptable amount of fat is restored, the body resumes its function.

One day a concerned mother brought her twenty-year-old normal-weight daughter in to see me. The girl was super-slender and had contracted many viral infections that winter. The mother was worried that her daughter's nutrition was poor, even though the girl ate balanced meals. I only had to ask one question of the daughter to know she was nutritionally fine. "Are your periods regular?" "Like clockwork," she said.

I assured both mother and daughter that nutrition wasn't the answer. It turned out that the girl had a lot of seasonal allergies that were weakening her resistance to infection, and shots cleared the problem up.

Libido

Women definitely feel sexier when they diet. Fat supports estrogen, which is a mothering type of hormone. Once you lose it, the male hormones come through a little stronger and you burn at a higher flame. Not to mention that your body looks better and you're apt to feel more agile.

The male libido, however, often hangs by a fragile metabolic thread. Ketosis sometimes leaves men eager but impotent, and then panic sets in. Even I, the doctor, have been caught up in the hysteria; once I tried to concoct ginseng root potions for my newly lean but not libidinous male patients. I stopped that craziness when I realized I could make men potent again by adding back what I'd originally taken away—carbohydrates!

Weight-Loss Patterns

Few things depress me as much as patients who compare their weight loss to their friends' weight loss. "Jane lost eight pounds and I only lost five," a woman will announce, and sulk.

"But you are forty years old, five-foot-two, and inactive," I'll protest. "Jane is five-foot-seven, thirty years old, and skis on weekends."

"Oh," she'll say. "You mean that makes a difference?"

If you are a twenty-five-year-old, five-foot-seven underburning female, you cannot compare yourself to a:

twenty-five-year-old, five-foot-seven *male* underburner;
twenty-five-year-old, five-foot-seven female *normalweight,*
twenty-five-year-old, five-foot-seven *male normalweight,*
thirty-five-year-old, five-foot-*three* female underburner.

You *can* compare yourself to a five-foot-seven underburning female who is exactly your weight and build, has followed your identical diet and exercise pattern, has not dieted in the past year, and is in the same state of health as you are. Which means you really can't compare yourself to anyone.

Weight losses for underburners all have a way of evening out. The differences are usually accounted for by the number of calories they consume. The normal diet of 1,200 calories or above will net losses of eight to twelve pounds a month; the low-calorie diet of 750 to 999 calories, ten to twenty pounds a month; and the very low calorie diet of less than 700 calories, fifteen to thirty pounds a month. The female underburner is going to lose on the lower end of this scale.

Getting bent out of shape if you don't lose what you think you should lose is self-defeating. If you follow instructions and hang in there, the pounds will come off, and a month more or less won't make any difference in the long run. In fact, if my patients finish a diet around the Christmas season, I keep them on it for four more weeks because it's such a difficult season to start maintenance.

There are some weeks you will diet perfectly and nothing will happen, and others when you won't work as hard and will lose perfectly.

You might get excited one week because you lost a big chunk of weight, and the next be devastated because your body has corrected itself and you've lost nothing. It's all part of the game.

The Plateau

A plateau is a stage in a diet when reduced eating and increased exercise bring no results. It's frustrating as hell: *You're* holding up your end of the bargain (by not eating the things you want to eat), but your body lets you down.

The main cause of a plateau is fluid retention. It's much more common in females and can occur premenstrually, at ovulation, with certain drugs, and with the ingestion of slightly more salt than normal. Usually, the plateau will end within ten days. If you can't wait, try some vitamin B_6 (300 mg), or sharply decrease your carbohydrates for one day only. (Limit yourself to three small cans of tuna.) Of course, if your plateau is premenstrual, you must wait until your period. You'll lose water the day before you lose blood, and most of the fluid retention will be gone by the time you start menstruating.

If low salt, menses, or the protein day do not budge your weight, you're faced with the second reason for the plateau—a drop in thyroid, which I explain in detail in Chapter 15, pages 131–135.

The third reason for the plateau is that you've reached your set-point weight. It might be ten or fifteen pounds higher than you thought it was, but no amount of exercise, thyroid, or protein days will do any permanent good.

Redistribution

It would be nice if you could lose weight in the most troublesome spots first. But your body has weird ideas about where it's appropriate to dump fat. The body will never judge beauty pageants. It often leaves you with a thin face, scrawny neck, and hollow clavicles, as well as unsightly lumps around the thighs and a bulge in the lower abdomen. But you've lost as much as you can or want, so what do you do?

You wait. This fat can be remarkably resistant to normal breakdown, but *redistribution* will eventually take place. Patience. Six weeks after a successful diet, your face will fill out and your lumps will empty; your figure will look quite different without further weight loss.

Chapter 13
BAN THE BINGE

As I've suggested all along, the major problem with low-starch diets—besides boring food—is that they can be very unsatisfying. Since the underburner has a larger food capacity, the empty feeling that follows a balanced-diet meal is often murder to live with. "The Craving" pays a call on every dieter, sooner or later. And the majority—even the most dedicated—don't survive the visit. Satisfying the craving with fatty sweets or starches (often the easiest, tastiest, and most available) will result in a weight gain that's not proportional to the amount of calories consumed. This is the end of the line and triggers the "feeding frenzy" or "binge."

If you ignore the craving and eat something like protein (as in meat), fructose (as in fruit), or salad (as in lettuce), you'll have eaten all those things and still have the craving. You'll still want that carbofat.

In my first book, I invented something called the "Cheat List" that I realize now is all wrong. The theory sounded good. If you just *had* to binge, and you just *had* to have a cookie—which was number 22 on the list—you were required to eat the twenty-one things that came before it. Those twenty-one things began with raw vegetables and worked their way up, logically, through eggs, hard cheese, fish, meat, cold cuts, and so on. I figured that by the time most dieters got to number 8 or 9 on the list, they'd be so filled up they'd stop right there. I thought volume alone would satisfy a craving. The problem was that no one was ever satisfied until they got to the carbohydrates at the end—so they ate their way through unnecessary calories first.

Now I think the craving comes from frustrated carbohydrate receptors that are looking for a fix. The trick is how to give it to them without triggering a binge. I find that mashed, butter-flavored, semi-starch vegetables fill that emptiness fast—mashed turnips, sweet and sour cabbage, and spaghetti squash parmesan. When I diet I always have a turnip, spaghetti squash, or cabbage nearby. I alternate every week so I don't get tired of my snack.

Here is my new list, altered for the 1980s. It speaks to what really ails you, and it still keeps those cookies at the end, far out of reach.

The New Binge List

1. Raw vegetables
2. Cooked vegetables (See above.)
3. Fruit
4. Plain popcorn
5. Rice
6. High-fiber bread
7. Potatoes—plain, boiled, or baked
8. Noodles with plain marinara sauce
9. Skim milk or Alba
10. Cottage cheese
11. Plain yogurt with or without fruit
12. Canned fruits without sugar
13. Eggs
14. Meat, plain
15. Fruit juice
16. Ice milk or sherbet
17. Crackers
18. Hard cheese
19. Ice cream
20. Nuts
21. Fried foods
22. Cakes
23. Pies
24. Cookies

Chapter 14

MAINTENANCE

And the Fight Goes On

There are two phases of a successful diet: weight loss and maintenance. The weight-loss phase is simplest. You follow instructions, live with your cravings, and in exchange enjoy the thrill of your clothes growing stylishly baggy and your friends more envious. But a weight-loss diet teaches you nothing except how to lose weight. A maintenance diet, on the other hand, teaches you how to eat.

The dramatic part is over; now the real work begins.

Early Maintenance
(From the day your diet ends until the fifth month)

Month One

When they finish a diet, most people have a prompt three-or-four-pound water-weight gain, now known, appetizingly, as "refeeding edema." The water's an old friend—it's what you lost at the beginning of the diet. Once you start eating carbohydrates, it always comes back, because carbofats and fatcarbos attract it like crazy (that's one reason carbos muck up weight loss). There's also retention in the liver, which restocks itself with glycogen (a starchlike substance that's changed into a sugar). The glycogen pulls in water to prepare for normal, non-weight-loss living. It's homecoming day in your body.

If you refeed correctly, though, you don't have to gain weight. When you lose fat, your body holds water for a short time simply to maintain volume, so there's always a lag between the actual burning and the drop in scale weight. Which means that when you finish a diet, your body still owes you a few pounds. So if you refeed slowly (in other words, you don't pig out your first week off the diet), the water your body releases and the water it picks up will cancel each other out.

You still have to stick to your basic weight-loss diet, but things ease up considerably. Add one starch at one meal per day. One starch means *one* of the following: 1 piece of bread, 1/2 cup rice, 1 potato, 1/2 sweet potato, 1/2 cup pasta, 1 tortilla, 1/4 sheet matzo, 1/2 bagel, 1/2 roll, 1 small pita bread, or 1/2 cup bulgur. Allow yourself more of foods like salad and cooked vegetables and an ounce more of protein.

Weigh yourself *every morning,* right after you've emptied your bladder. Record your weight. If you gain more than two pounds in a day, return to the weight-loss version of your diet. Lesser gains usually just mean fluid retention.

The worst thing you can do is avoid the scale. That way lies madness, or at least fatness.

If you do put on those two pounds or more, record and review the foods that made you gain so quickly. After you've lost the weight, return to the maintenance plan but omit the offending substances.

I always tell dieters not to exercise too frenetically at the beginning of their weight-loss program, because they'll have to increase their movement in maintenance. That's because the basal metabolic rate drops with dieting, so if you start out too vigorously you'll have nowhere to go, and you won't be able to counteract the metabolic slowdown. It's yet another reason for rapid regain in maintenance. Even though I advocate four walks a week, I often start my patients out with just two in the first month, three in the second, and four—finally—in the third. The first month of maintenance, I increase the number of walks to *five* and drop back to four after that, when I'm sure their weight isn't creeping insidiously up.

Needless to say, if underburners expect to get thin and stay thin, exercise will have to be an integral part of their lives.

Month Two

Again, *weigh yourself daily.* Follow the same rules as above.

After the first month is over, you may *cautiously* add one sugar, two times a week. A sugar can be either a dessert (such as ice cream) or a main course (such as sweet and sour chicken). Add this only on the condition that no more is available for leftovers—no quarts of ice cream in your freezer, no slices of pie in your fridge. It's not that I don't trust you; it's that I don't trust your carbohydrate receptors. So I encourage you to eat your sugar when you're away from home.

You may also add one tablespoon of fat daily as a dressing, a garnish, or for frying. However, you cannot add this fat when you eat out. In most restaurants, they don't know the meaning of the word *dry,* so assume you're getting it anyway.

I used to allow a lot of free foods between meals, but I've come to the conclusion that nibbling in and of itself is fattening. Sure, you might start out with carrots, pickles, lettuce leaves, and rice cakes, but someday, when none of that stuff is around, you'll opt for real food. However, I'll let you have one pick-me-up, not to exceed 30 calories, in the midafternoon and evening. Underburners should do their serious eating at meals only.

I have no problem with artificial sweeteners, provided new research doesn't show them to be more dangerous than we already know they are. Nutrasweet and its ilk can make a lot of low-calorie foods more palatable, and you shouldn't let normalweights harass you for sweetening fruit, cereal, or even salad if your dressing is a little too vinegary. If you find, however, that low-calorie sweeteners are giving you too much of a sweet tooth, you might want to cut down.

If behavior modification has a function anywhere, it's in maintenance. It will also be hard to restrain yourself; perhaps you'll have better luck if you can *retrain* yourself. Part of that retraining is learning where to save calories.

As an underburner, you burn about 700 calories a day less than your normalweight peers; and in maintenance, you have to make up that difference. You can try to do it with exercise, but it would take an enormous commitment to burn that many calories. It's much easier to do with food substitutions.

Take salad dressing. If an underburner has two large salads per day and puts three or four tablespoons of regular dressing on each, he'll have consumed 300 calories from the dressing alone. If he switches to a diet dressing, he'll knock off 200 calories (also a lot of flavor, probably, but there are ways of spiking up diet dressing with herbs, seasonings, and low-calorie sweeteners).

A three-egg omelet made with two whole eggs and one egg white (fried in a no-stick pan) saves 150 calories.

A baked potato and a tablespoon of cottage cheese—instead of sour cream—saves 40 calories.

Low-fat cottage cheese saves 50 calories; skim milk, 70; sugarless gum, 20 per stick; thin-sliced bread, 20; plain yogurt, 80; and diet Jell-O, 60.

I could go on and on, but you get the idea.

Just for fun, think about the food you ate today or yesterday and find the 700 hidden calories you could have cut.

Month Three

Again, weigh yourself daily. Same rules.

If your cholesterol is normal, you may be slightly more liberal with meat now, in both amount and preparation. Two times a week you can have a fancy or sauced meat dish *(not* to be combined with a sweet dessert). You can also start substituting vegetable proteins for meat; legumes, peas, lentils, and tofu can make for interesting main-course dishes. But remember to use them as meat *replacements,* not sidekicks.

Let's have a frank talk about cheese. Unless you're going to call it a meal, there's no place in an underburner's life for cheese and crackers. Cheese can be substituted for meat at this point, but think of it as a fatty meat (almost 70 percent fat, in fact). So if fat is a problem, you'd better stick to skim milk, cottage cheese, or yogurt. Peanut butter is also a fatty protein, but at least the fat part doesn't have cholesterol.

Since underburners can't eat as much real food as they need to fill them up, they must learn the art of diluting (as opposed to concentrating) calories. That means no fruit juice or dried fruit, even if it's healthful; you simply lose too much of the filling power.

Consider the grape: one tablespoon of raisins packs in 60 calories; a few swallows of grape juice supply even more in less space. The grape itself isn't so terrific for underburners—you can eat it too fast, and it's not all that filling. An enterprising diet group has suggested putting it in the freezer, and I think the result makes a neat dessert: frozen grapes, more filling than raisins, more exotic than grape juice, and more challenging to eat than the grape at room temperature. You have to think like this all the time if you want to maintain your weight.

In the original version of the Pinocchio story, the hungry puppet was given two pears. He peeled and ate them—leaving a substantial amount of skin and, around the core, flesh—but was still hungry. Jiminy Cricket advised him to eat the rest.

"No one eats the skin!" said Pinocchio, outraged.

"Then stay hungry!" said the cricket.

Pinocchio ended up eating not just the skin but also the flesh he had left *and* the rind. He was satisfied.

Jiminy Cricket was one of our first behavior-modification counselors. He understood that eating the whole fruit, including the fiber and fluid, is how you make your calories go the farthest. It's how nature intended fruit to be consumed.

Cooked or canned fruit loses some of its water and most of its fiber. Avoid the canned stuff, which often has added sugar. The only time I eat cooked fruit is when I'm desperate for a different taste, and even then I leave the skin on and undercook it: the crisp baked apple, the slightly poached pear, the broiled grapefruit. I'll also make simple fruit sauces to give fresh fruit a little glamour—strawberry purée over raspberries, blueberry sauce over melon, or minced peaches on a sliced banana.

The idea is to dilute a higher calorie substance with a lower calorie one. A traditional chicken salad made with one cup diced chicken, two tablespoons of mayonnaise, and two tablespoons of chopped celery is about 450 calories. And you're still hungry. If you use one tablespoon of diet mayonnaise, increase the celery to a half-cup, and add a cup of shredded romaine lettuce, you've more than doubled the volume of your salad but the calories have dropped to 300. You've also decreased fat and added a little more fiber.

Dilution tricks are fun, and you're only limited by your imagination. When you want a tasty carbohydrate but not the calories, brown rice diluted with vegetables works splendidly. Any meat can be diluted in a stir fry with vegetables, making two ounces look like a large portion. (Alone on a plate it would look pitiful.) Shredding helps. In a chef's salad, it makes an ounce of meat and cheese go a long way; and one slice of broiled pepperoni, finely chopped, can add a lot of flavor to low-calorie eggplant Parmesan.

In fact, you only need small amounts of full-flavored substances like olive oil, sesame seeds, and caviar. A tablespoon of grated strong cheese, such as Parmesan or blue, does wonders for a low-calorie salad dressing.

Month Four

By now you can eat most of what your family and friends eat, so you don't have to feel left out. Thanks to record keeping and daily weighing, you should know which foods are trouble. Keeping that in mind, you can start to prepare more complex recipes. Experiment by cutting the fat in half and substituting low-calorie margarine, milk, mayonnaise, and sour cream. I now cook Chinese food with a fraction of a recipe's oil, and the results are terrific.

Remember to *exercise, exercise, exercise* to bring that citrate oxidase and lipoprotein lipase down. Those are the enzymes that urge your fat cells to fill up again after they've emptied. In normalweights, these levels drop naturally as weight is lost; but in underburners, they stay elevated much longer. Exercise is how you bring them down.

More Good Food Stuff

Soup, if it's low calorie, can be a filler both in diet and maintenance. Accompanied by a salad and fruit (forget the bread, there's plenty of starch in the soup), it can even be a meal. Every hungry person should keep a container of clear, low-calorie broth in the refrigerator for that 4:00 to 6:00 P.M. "hungry hour." Keep it simple. Take a canned broth (College Inn is good), skim off the fat, and add a low-calorie food: chicken broth with mushrooms, spinach, and water chestnuts, or chopped fresh tomatoes and scallions; tomato broth with mushrooms, a drop of Tabasco, or a dollop of fresh chopped cucumbers.

My son, observing me toss the ends of asparagus down the disposal, said, "What are you doing? If you cook them for half an hour and purée them, they make a great soup base." I followed his advice, boiled tough asparagus stems in beef bouillon, puréed them, and added the purée to a thin, rather uninteresting tomato broth. It was marvelous.

I am continually amazed by how badly most restaurants prepare gazpacho, which is low in calories and delicious. It's also easy to make. Take four cups of Bloody Mary mix (without alcohol) or plain tomato juice and add half a green pepper, half a red pepper, half a peeled cucumber, one fresh tomato (peeled), and two cloves of chopped garlic. If you're not using the Bloody Mary mix, season it to taste. Blend or process the soup until it's thick but still chunky. I add onion to each portion individually because if you make it ahead, the onion tends to be overpowering. A friend of mine does it more simply—she takes today's leftover salad and purées it for tomorrow's soup. Cold soup can also be made by poaching vegetables like spinach, cucumbers, and zucchini in bouillon and puréeing them. You can add a tablespoon of plain yogurt for richness.

If you're using soup as a filler, it should stay below 60 calories a cup or you'll have to eat it as a main course or substitute it for fruit.

Middle Maintenance
(From month five to year two)
Rules to live by:

1. Continue to exercise at least fifteen minutes daily and to walk forty minutes four times a week.
2. Watch that 4:00 to 6:00 P.M. hunger period. If you're at home, prepare the meal earlier so you're out of the kitchen by four. If you have to, prepare most of supper after lunch.
3. Avoid night eating, even of low-calorie foods.
4. Avoid snacks in cellophane bags. Avoid cellophane bags.
5. Avoid fast-food restaurants unless they have salad bars.
6. Avoid most vending machines.
7. Operate on the assumption that you can find some type of diet food even in the greasiest spoon. Don't say, "What the hell. When in Rome . . ."
8. Don't be afraid to tell restaurants how you want it: "dry," "with dressing on the side," "without the sauce," and so on. Restaurant owners want people to keep eating out, so they're alert to changing needs.

9. When you party or eat out, choose between consuming your calories in food or in alcoholic beverages.

10. Carry emergency supplies with you. Diet salad dressing, diet soda, and even water-packed tuna can help if you're famished.

11. If you overeat, and you will occasionally (it's human nature), total the calories of your episode and subtract them from your next three days' maintenance allowance. If you must binge, binge sensibly. (See my Binge List, page 108.)

I don't want to start a battle with gourmet husbands or eager-to-please wives (or vice versa), but if underburners insist on surrounding themselves with tempting food, they'll never, never stay thin. One patient told me she loved to cook and just had to make fancy dishes every night for her husband and kids. The list of her recent culinary triumphs nearly had me drooling, and it also convinced me she'd never lose weight (or if, by some miracle, she did, she'd never keep it off). I was right.

Let me tell you about two caterers, Alice and Betty. Alice was thin and Betty was heavy. People used to say that Alice was active and burned off all her calories, while Betty was slow and tasted everything she cooked. The sad truth was that Alice constantly tasted her own food and was less active than Betty, who worked another full-time job and ruthlessly limited her tastings. The moral of my story is: "Only normalweights should be caterers."

Certain food situations will always create problems for underburners. Carbofat leftovers will always beckon, especially around Thanksgiving and Christmas. (This is why publishers like to release their diet books in January.) When you have tempting leftovers, save a few pieces only if your family really wants them. Then give the rest away.

Some Special Occasions

The Sick Underburner

If you have an illness or surgery that lays you up, take a little extra zinc and protein for the healing process, along with a good multivitamin, but watch your calories carefully. The underburner needs to expend energy to prevent weight gain, even with normal eating, so if you're ill and bedridden, you need *very* little food. This is when many underburners get fatter than ever, gaining as much as twenty pounds because they think it will help them get their strength back. But they have plenty of energy stored in their fat.

The experts tell us the body requires 1,100 calories just to breathe, but I think an inactive underburner needs about half that. That's a few cups of chicken soup, some soda crackers, a little orange juice, and some Coke syrup to settle the tum. Actually, there's enough carbohydrate in all that not only to stop weight loss but to start weight gain. Suffering, unfortunately, uses up very few of the underburner's calories.

Yet most sick people are advised to eat:

"You need your strength."

"This is no time to watch your weight."

"Have a little toast and butter. You need something in your stomach."

"Ice cream will soothe your throat."

Even if the underburner has nausea and vomiting—and his stomach is *begging* for a rest—the food deliverers feel they must force-feed. I'm not just talking about mothers and loving spouses here; doctors are just as bad. It's as if we were suddenly transported to the dark ages, when we only had food and leeches to treat an illness. I can't tell you how many times I've heard competent physicians tell obese patients with uncomplicated viruses, "Forget about your weight; you need good, nourishing food."

I've seen too many physicians treat underburners with fruit juices, honey, crackers, Coke syrup, cough medicines loaded with sugar (you can take them in pill form, and underburners should) and—horror of horrors—ice cream for sore throats. This is advice for *normalweights:* Sick underburners should be told to drink low-calorie fluids and bouillon, to eat diet Jell-O, to take vitamin pills, and, for a sore throat, to suck on an ice cube.

People suffer an average of two or three temporary illnesses a year. If they gain two pounds each time, that makes six unnecessary pounds. You'll recover just fine without high-calorie carbofats, and when you're out of bed, you won't look into the mirror and want to cry.

The Vacationing Underburner

If you have to diet for a long time, your diet will always interfere with your vacations (and vice versa). Underburners usually hold their weight rather well on trips. One reason is that they move more; another is that they do less private eating, which is always the biggest danger.

I think it's a mistake to diet too rigidly on a vacation, because you always end up feeling sorry for yourself and then indulging when you get home. So I've devised a set of instructions for my vacationing patients, just so they don't forget me.

1. If you're going where the food is unique and famous, for goodness sake eat it once so you don't turn into a martyr. That means Maryland crab cakes, Texas barbecue, New Orleans oysters, Maine lobster, and so on. (Pennsylvania shoofly pie isn't worth the calories.)

2. If you're going somewhere you can pack food—on a camping or boating trip, for instance. Diet food is as easy to pack as anything.

3. If you're traveling by car, stock it with nonperishables and periodically stop for fruit or vegetables. If you stop for fast food, make sure there's a salad bar. It would be a shame to gain your vacation weight on fast food.

4. If you choose to go on a cruise during a diet, you never were serious about the diet in the first place, no matter what your reason. ("My husband booked it because he doesn't want to be near a telephone," is the most common.) On cruises they serve food constantly, and you don't get much exercise.

5. Go to countries where you know the food is terrible, like Russia, Ireland, China, England, Scotland, Africa, Greece, or Disneyland. And stick to the plainest dishes you can find.

6. Go to countries where you lose more food than you take in —not necessarily from the same orifice. Mexico and Egypt come painfully to mind.

7. Try vacationing in New York. The prices are so high and the portions so small that it's difficult to get enough food. Once I was so hungry I chewed an inedible leaf under a miniscule piece of salmon.

8. Avoid prepaid meal plans. If you're subscribing to save money, try to make up the difference by eating less.
9. No eating between meals. No booze between meals either.
10. Learn how to order—you can instruct anyone how to serve or prepare anything. I once explained to a Greek omelet chef how to make mine without oil. He didn't speak a word of English, and I didn't speak a word of Greek.
11. Remember to walk, walk, walk—the beach, the desert, the deck, the mountain, the street market.

Bon Voyage.

Late Maintenance
(Two years and over)

If you have kept your weight down for two years, congratulations. There's a chance you've altered your metabolism and can gain more like a normalweight—about a pound a month or twelve pounds a year, a manageable figure. (Underburners, remember, can gain five or more pounds a month, which adds up to sixty-plus a year.)

Exercise, preventive dieting, and regular weighing are the building blocks of a healthy, normalweight future.

The Starvation Syndrome

Often the price of maintaining cosmetic thinness for the underburner is to live in a state of semistarvation. At one point in my practice, I thought I was running a workshop for Diet Club owners. About five women who owned, managed, or worked in various clubs in the area came to me as patients. Their complaints were similar. Each had gotten thin on the Diet Club's regimen, invested in the franchise, and made diet their livelihood. But in order to maintain the thin image necessary for business, they were forced to starve themselves.

By the time I saw them, they were sick and tired of their chain's special filet of sole, chicken breasts, and special bran muffins. Day and night, they thought of nothing but food; they even dreamed about food. They were irritable, hungry, depressed, and constantly bingeing. They begged me to help them keep their weight off. If these leaders in the diet field couldn't maintain thinness—with all the positive reinforcements they had—how could the average dieter expect to do better?

This illustrates the plight of many women who have lost considerable amounts of weight and now have to live a spartan existence to keep it off. Regain is not always caused by going back to bad eating habits. Sometimes it's just the failure to be unreasonably hard on yourself. In other words, it's human.

Maintaining Thinness for Life

The psychology of thinness can be reduced to five important principles. If you learn them, your fight will be easier, if only because you won't be in the dark.

1. The Narcissistic Principle. You have to be into your body. Really into it. You have to take care of it, clothe it, and love it; or you have to be into the body of someone who doesn't want you to be fat.

2. The Walk-Don't-Read Principle. Education is great, but save the books and magazines for late at night when you're not going anywhere. Spend your free time walking, running, or playing a sport.

3. The Planning Principle. The world caters to normalweights, so you have to plan a strategy daily to avoid being placed in compromising (high-calorie) positions.

4. The Purifying Principle. Like it or not, you'll spend a lot of your time hungry. Learn to live with it. Think of it as a purifying experience.

5. The Mind-Over-Matter Principle. Remember, your body wants you to be plump, and so your mind must always fight for you to be thin. If you were a genetically fat rat with a tiny brain, you'd have no choice in the matter. But you have read this book. And you know the fight goes on.

Chapter 15

HELPING THE UNDERBURNER

Controlling Your Intake

Diet Pills

The way to keep people on a diet, science has always assumed, is to kill their hunger. Logical enough, but try defining human hunger. (I have, and, like you, I'm not satisfied with the definition.) Most experiments involve animal hunger, which is all very fine except that white rats, even fat ones, don't lie awake at night longing for hot-fudge sundaes. A few years ago, someone came up with a diet pill that worked incredibly well on cats. The word was: *This is the diet pill to end all diet pills.* Ads showed pictures of a kitty turning his whiskers up at a dish of gourmet cat food. I don't know if it's still available for obese cats, but on humans it was a dismal failure.

The diet pill has been the most promising tool in the quest to control a person's hunger. If you're forced to reduce your calories below 1,000 a day to lose weight, it stands to reason you'll be hungry. And it also stands to reason that if there's a relatively safe and effective pill to make you less hungry, it would be intelligent, humane, and medically ethical to give it to you, under close medical supervision—provided your intent is not to abuse the pill but to use it to decrease your food intake. This is all straightforward enough, but the history of diet pills has been fraught with scandal and abuse.

The initial pills, the amphetamines, suppressed hunger by working on the neurochemical transmitters of the brain. You lost weight all right, but once you went off the pills, your hunger returned with a vengeance, so you gained it all back and then some. The problem was no one wanted to stop taking them.

Physicians themselves were largely responsible for the rapid demise of amphetamines, which were, at least initially, effective diet pills. Doctors gave them out too casually, in too large quantities, without adequate supervision or diet instructions. People would use them up, not bother to eat, and then, left without pills and with a ravenous hunger to replace what they'd lost, eat every carbofat and fatcarbo in sight. They learned nothing about dieting on amphetamines; all they learned was that the pill made them speedy and anorexic, and often euphoric. So they'd return to their doctor and beg for more pills—a request that was usually granted. Then the whole foolish cycle would start over again. Used indiscriminately, the pill would burn people out. Ultimately, it made them paranoid, exhausted, depressed.

The drug manufacturers, sensing disaster, came up with a diluted amphetamine, stripped of most of its tumultuous side effects. These anorectic agents answer to names like Fastin, Ionamine (phentermine), Sanorex (mazindol), Plegine, Prelu 2 (phendimetrazine), and Tenuate (diethylpropion hydrochloride).

Another distant relative to amphetamines is the over-the-counter diet pill, composed of a chemical called phenylpropylalanine, which is used curiously enough as a nasal decongestant. (I used to wonder why I wasn't hungry when I took a cold tablet; I thought the cold had killed my appetite.) These pills have a mild appetite-suppressing effect but a strong tendency to make you jittery and irritable. They've also been criticized because they're available to everyone, which means there's the real risk of someone with heart disease, hypertension, or on a noncompatible medication gobbling them down. And going into cardiac arrest.

For a while, I staunchly defended the use of the anorectic diet pills as an adjunct to a total program. I reasoned that underburners need all the help they can get on a grueling weight-loss plan; watching my patients suffer, I couldn't imagine a good enough reason to deny them some relief. Then I found one: The pills don't really work. Oh, they're fine pills, and they do what they're supposed to do. The trouble is much less surmountable: human nature.

One of the reasons it's so frustrating to practice diet medicine is that the responsibility for success ultimately rests on the dieter. In traditional medicine, the doctor treats the patient with pills and makes him feel better. In diet medicine, the doctor guides and instructs the patient, but the patient must do the work. Most patients are not ready to accept this responsibility for their health care. So they tend to overestimate the importance of any pill they're given. Thus, they take the poor diet pill—intended only to decrease physical hunger—and rely on it to do all the work.

Hunger, however, is a basic drive, as basic as reproduction, and you'd need more than a pill to kill it completely. (Using a diet pill to eliminate hunger is a little like using saltpeter to stop the sex drive, the way the army did once for our boys overseas. It didn't work there, either.) After the initial shock of not being hungry, the body figures out ways to get around the diet pill, which grows increasingly less effective. And a diet pill can do nothing about *appetite,* the longing for specific foods. Underburners get fat not from the *I needs* but the *I wants:* "I want ice cream, I want cookies, I want a cheeseburger and french fries." No diet pill in the world will keep pudgy fingers off a chocolate chip cookie. So if the motivation to diet is not exceedingly high, the patient fails and blames the pill.

"Jeez, Doc, that pill didn't work at all. I was still hungry."

"But Al, you can eat all the salad you want . . ."

"But I don't *want* salad, Doc."

When patients don't remove themselves from the source of temptation, relying on their diet pills to carry them through, they're doomed to failure. Often they end up nibbling high-calorie foods as they did before the diet and taking a diet pill *in addition.* When you remove their chemical crutch, they eat the foods they like in larger quantities, which leads to bingeing and immediate weight gain. At this point, even the most idealistic doctor must ask, "What good are diet pills in the first place?"

Having asked that, I'm still unwilling to condemn them out of hand. Their addictive potential is not as strong in the underburner, who'd rather eat than take pills any day. What we should be doing is finding selective, creative uses for them, with full knowledge of their strengths and limitations. How about considering them:

1. For a short time at the beginning of a diet, when you're trying to muzzle your unrestrained eating.
2. For vacations, when temptation levels are extremely high.
3. At the end of an excruciatingly long diet, when willpower is exhausted.
4. In early maintenance, when the urge to overeat is tremendous, as the body tries to refill its fat cells.

I began to think of diet pills for maintenance when I saw three patients in a row who'd lost enormous amounts of weight with no problems, only to return the same year with more than half of that weight regained. It's easy to do that. Relatively few calories and/or carbohydrates are needed to open up newly closed fat cells; certain hormone levels are decreased in response to weight loss; and, finally, there is a spectacular appetite rebound.

You have a few options for reducing your appetite in this situation. One is a low carbohydrate diet, which will get you into ketosis (the metabolic state conducive to fat burning) pretty fast. Another is to start exercising a lot. Another is to use over-the-counter appetite suppressants (without caffeine). But if all these methods fail, is it better to try a mild diet pill or to eat back to your former weight? I ask; I do not know.

Like all my patients, I still entertain the hope that a pill will someday cure obesity. In the past few years, natural amino acids (proteins) such as tryptophan, and amino acid-containing foods—such as spirolina, a green algae—have been attracting some attention, spurred on, I'm sure, by large numbers of nonmedical people now involved in the treatment of obesity. Amino acids are used to change the brain chemicals thought to stimulate appetite. The diet pill Pondimin (fenfluramine) acts similarly, but unlike tryptophan and spirolina, which are available in health-food stores, it's a prescription drug.

Pondimin raises brain serotonin levels and is supposed to cut hunger *and* depression. It also aids sleep. It might even help people burn fat. The problem is that it isn't such a great appetite suppressant. But the principle behind it will be the basis of a whole new line of diet pills. I'm not sure how effective they'll be, but I am excited that at last we'll have an anti-depressant that won't make you gain weight.

Suggestion

There are a few other hunger-controlling methods that deserve mention, but I don't think most of them are better than a mild diet pill or—I cringe to say it—willpower. They're certainly more expensive and complicated.

Hypnosis is a state of increased suggestibility. Most people are fascinated by it, thanks to stories about mad hypnotists and the pretty young things who do their bidding. The reality is less dramatic. "I didn't think I was hypnotized, but my therapist insisted I was," said one of my friends. (That's what hypnotists always say to people who aren't hypnotized.) "Anyway," she continued, "I lost six pounds."

My answer was "You probably weren't hypnotized, but you *wanted* to diet, so you went ahead and lost weight. Nothing wrong with that."

Hypnosis can be a valuable tool in psychotherapy. It's useful in dredging up painful events you've repressed over the years. But for changing your eating habits, it leaves a lot to be desired. Underburners don't give up control of their eating so easily.

I'm also unimpressed with the role of acupuncture in curbing hunger, although I think it does have merit in treating chronic pain. However, if someone truly believes that either of these methods is going to help him lose weight, then it just might—that's the power of increased suggestibility.

Hormone Shots

If you wait long enough, everything comes back into fashion. The first year I practiced diet medicine, I heard about a magical diet that used Chorionic Gonadotropin, the hormone from the urine of a pregnant horse. It was the rage in California and Florida. You received a daily injection in your buttocks, and this was supposed to depress your appetite, reduce the fat stores in your fattest spots (like the hips) *first,* and make you look terrific while you were losing weight.

The only catch was that the injection had to be accompanied by a 500-calorie, absolutely fat-free diet. You couldn't even use cream on your face, or handle something greasy unless you wore gloves. The program consisted of six weeks of daily injections (except for Sunday, a day of rest for both patient and doctor), six weeks of maintenance, another six weeks of daily injections, and so on until you lost as much as you wanted.

The opponents of this diet argued that anyone could lose weight on 500 calories a day. But its champions claimed that the injection killed your appetite completely and made it *possible* for you to follow the 500-calorie diet. More important, they said, it made you lose weight selectively and feel euphoric. There was a grain of truth in some of the claims (your skin looked good), but nowhere near enough to merit a sore behind, starvation, and the cost of the shots.

A mere fifteen years later, I heard one of my patients raving about this wonderful new diet from Florida where you got daily injections and the fat just melted off your hips and legs. "I'll bet it's the placental hormone from a pregnant horse," I mused. "How did you guess?" she asked, awed.

Some new hormones and enzymes for decreasing appetite are being investigated. These include Cholecystokinen (CCK), Pancreozymin, Thyrotropic Releasing Hormone (TRH), and Somatostatin.

CCK is a gastrointestinal hormone that among other things, slows the rate at which your stomach empties. This could act as an early "I'm full" signal to your brain and help you eat less. It's been successfully tested on rats, and preliminary reports say it might be more effective on men than on women. TRH comes from the pituitary gland and stimulates TSH, which in turn stimulates the thyroid gland. It's been shown to block the effect of beta endorphins in the brain, which means you eat less.

Have you heard of the frog diet? Well, just give it time to catch on. This diet will have to include frog skin, because bombesin, a substrate in it, lowers appetite. Possible side effects? That's easy to predict. Lowered voice, spasms of hopping, fondness for lily pads. But it will be worth it to be thin.

Exercise

Exercise can diminish hunger. I used to think it increased hunger, but recent studies suggest that's only true in brief and/or mild types of exercise. In sustained exercise (thirty minutes or more), actual metabolic and hormonal changes are taking place that do make you want to eat less.

The first metabolic change is a ketosis that occurs if fat reserves are being used without sufficient carbohydrate intake. This gives rise to anorexia (loss of appetite). It's the mechanism for appetite control in the high protein–low carbohydrate and semistarvation diets. Exercise also increases the breakdown product of muscles—lactic acid—and the "acidosis" suppresses your appetite. Finally, there are some interesting, though speculative, studies on long-distance runners. Research has suggested that certain brain chemicals they secrete—enkephalins and beta endorphins—decrease appetite by blocking hunger messages to the brain.

Jaw Wiring

Jaw wiring has always seemed the ultimate torture. Its sole objective is to keep starving people from food, without trying to help them handle the hunger that makes them eat. Teeth wired shut (and armed with wirecutters, in case they vomit), these dieters are forced to go through life like chained mad dogs. They might be able to avoid food, but they also lose the ability to speak clearly. Usually, they have no diet plan, just a terse set of instructions beginning, "Be careful what you drink." But these prisoners can be cunning—if nothing else is around, a beer or a milk shake will do.

As far as I'm concerned, anyone who submits to jaw wiring should be committed, along with the people doing the wiring. It's a foolish escape from the responsibilities of rational dieting, and it leaves its victims with loose teeth and an overwhelming urge to eat.

Controlling Your Behavior

No discussion about controlling your intake would be complete without touching on behavior modification therapy (BMT), the diet messiah of the 1970s. It all started when some astute psychologists noticed that overweight people exhibited strange behavior when it came to eating: They nibbled instead of eating full meals, they chose sweets over nutritious foods, and so on. The psychologists felt that if this behavior were corrected, fat people would get thin automatically and stay thin naturally.

An elaborate plan was devised. One of the first tasks was to outlaw the word *diet,* because the concept provoked such negative feelings. The catch phrases were now "altering behavior" and "discontinuing fat-making habits."

If you joined the program, the first (and perhaps most useful) step was to make an extensive food diary, which would help you identify the behavior that led to overeating. Cues—specific events that made you seek out food—were identified, and you were given specific instructions on how to modify them. For instance, if you ate too much when you watched TV, the answer was to eat only in rooms with no TV. Or else to destroy your set.

Probably nowhere in diet history has this much fuss been made out of so little information. The behaviorists took a handful of principles, generated millions of words out of them, and claimed to have found the solution to obesity. Admittedly, there are good things to be learned from BMT. The diary is useful because it makes you aware of what the problem areas are. List-making of daily food intake can also be helpful, but usually not for long; I've found that after a couple of weeks, many list-makers forget their lists at home, and a lot of people stop making them after their first indiscretion. Most people can figure out when and where they're eating incorrectly without all the ritual, but the list is a good tool for teenagers and younger children.

As far as I'm concerned, there are four major behavioral problems with underburners. They are:

1. Irregular eating patterns
2. A preference for sweets
3. Eating too rapidly
4. Insufficient amount of the right exercise

I have never seen a fat person who eats only three meals a day. In fact, underburners' eating patterns are so bizarre that I think their *behavior* is controlled by their different hormonal environment. Underburners aren't hungry in the morning, sometimes even skip lunch, but when they get home from school or work, they can hardly wait to start munching carbohydrates. These foods undoubtedly act as a tension-releasing device, in the same way a drink helps some people.

They will then eat a normal supper but become hungry about an hour later and nibble all night until bedtime—even waking in the middle of the night to continue feeding. Interestingly enough, if they're required to eat breakfast and lunch, they still behave the same way.

Changing erratic eating patterns means programming mealtimes and intercepting food cues—the things that trigger people's eating. That's an incredibly hard job. If you don't believe me, here are the food cues I heard *in just one day* in my office:

"My husband was in the hospital."
"I have company from out of town."
"I went to a wedding."
"I had an operation."
"My knee is sore."
"I had tendonitis."
"There's a new boss at work, and I'm tense."
"My boyfriend left me."
"I got an 'F' on my math test."

The behavior of sweet lovers is not much easier to change. Even if they agree to give up sugar, they'll happily turn to other carbofats or fatcarbos. Behaviorists insist on teaching them to stop at one sweet, which as I suggested earlier, is next to impossible. Once you trigger those carbohydrate and sugar receptors, you're going to *have* to wire their jaws. Underburners can't stop at one where sugar is concerned.

Eating rapidly is the trait that behaviorists have the most fun with. They get to give advice like, "Chew your food twenty times," "Take a sip of water between bites," "Use chopsticks," and "Don't finish your meal before twenty minutes have elapsed." All that certainly takes the joy out of eating, and maybe that's just what underburners need. Unfortunately, it's not something they'll tolerate.

For every technique you supply, the determined eater has a way to dodge it. That's why behavior modification often breaks down into more game-playing for people who play games continually.

Patient: I eat all night!
Doctor: Eat only at the kitchen table.
Patient: Okay, I'll go to the kitchen table and eat all night.
Doctor: Stay out of the house at night.
Patient: I'll get food at a fast-food place.
Doctor: Don't go to fast-food places.
Patient: Then how can I stay out of the house at night?
Doctor: Go to the movies.
Patient: I eat junk at the movies.

Doctor: Don't buy junk.

Patient: I'll go crazy. What'll I do with my hands?

If you look carefully at what people are saying, you can see the seeds of their failure. For instance, one said to me recently, "I'm good at controlling my eating around people, but I'm terrible alone."

The obvious answer is "Don't be alone."

The obvious answer to the obvious answer is, "That's impossible."

The message implied by all this is, "It's impossible to diet."

The behaviorists don't understand the underburner, and what's more, they don't want to. They assume—and why shouldn't they, everyone else does—that the underburner has abnormal behavior compared to the rest of the world. In other words, normal portions, normal eating speed, normal chewing, and normal appetite are determined by people of normal weight.

Overweight normalweights do okay on behavior modification programs. In underburners, however, the metabolic state often influences the behavior, and until you can change the metabolism, you'll have a hell of a time changing the behavior. Underburners don't always exhibit enough bad behavior to explain the amount of adipose tissue they're carrying around.

So forget chewing twenty times or putting your knife and fork down between bites. That's kindergarten stuff, and the point is to make you more responsible about what you eat. The behavioral instructions for underburners should be:

Don't eat anything over 60 calories between meals.

Don't eat anything with a lot of sugar.

Slow down enough to taste your food.

Put physical distance between yourself and food.

Move as much as you can.

EXTRA! EXTRA! NEW BEHAVIORAL TECHNIQUE FROM THE UNITED KINGDOM!

After I wrote the above, I attended an international conference on obesity. For the final lecture, a learned Scottish professor reported on what he called "an exciting new behavioral method for controlling obesity."

Could this be the breakthrough we'd all been waiting for?

"It's a nylon cord knotted tightly around the waist," he continued. Yes, yes?

"That's all. We got the idea from models who went on holiday. They had gold chains soldered around their waist to keep them from gaining weight. But gold is a bit expensive, ya' know?"

Maybe chewing twenty times isn't such a bad idea.

Controlling Your Metabolism

Thyroid

More professionals are now willing to admit, although grudgingly, that there's a metabolic difference between normalweights and underburners. But nobody's sure what the difference is. It could be a substance secreted by the brain to protect fat or a defect in the fat cell itself. Perhaps it's too little of a hormone that breaks down fat, a sluggish pituitary gland, an enzyme disorder, a vitamin lack, an energy pump failing to function, and so on.

To most people, the word *metabolism* means thyroid function. If only thyroid were the cause of fatness—how easy it would be to cure! But no matter how hard we've tried, we can't find an absolute thyroid deficiency in most underburners.

The thyroid gland sits in the base of the neck and secretes two hormones, T_3 and T_4. Together these two have something to do with body temperature, body weight, muscle strength, and fluid balance (plus hundreds of other functions we know little about). There is four times as much T_4 as T_3, and they have different jobs in the body. T_4 is a more stable form of the hormone, just plodding along doing its mundane work. T_3 is young, vigorous, and about four times more active than T_4.

Thirty years ago, thyroid was the accepted treatment for any female who complained of fatigue, sensitivity to cold, excessive hair loss, or weight gain. The popular thyroid test was the BMR, a breathing test on which most women scored -20 (a value that supposedly indicated a deficiency in thyroid function). Actually, what that test revealed was that women in general have a lower body temperature at rest. As more sophisticated and accurate blood tests appeared, most women were shown to have perfectly normal thyroid glands, and that confirmed what the general public had always thought about obesity—that we were dealing with people who just overate.

So the last twenty years have been devoted to studying what sort of twisted psyches would lead fatties to endanger their lives, jeopardize their happiness, and mar their appearance with too much food. The answer, of course, was very twisted indeed. This viewpoint ushered in the "Dark Ages of Obesity" or the "Psychiatrist's Inquisition." Oh, it wasn't entirely the psychiatrists' fault; like many of their fellow physicians, they were relying on tests that showed a normal thyroid function. Even the most sensitive TSH (thyroid stimulating hormone) test failed to reveal that many underburners suffered from an underactive thyroid.

Little by little, the overweight American female has been weaned off her thyroid, and the outcry has been deafening. I don't know why: Thyroid almost never makes people skinny, even if they show a true deficiency. It does make most women feel more energetic and retain less fluid, but it's not the fat-burning pill it was once touted as. Fat people *feel* better, but they're still fat.

There are still thousands of women who take thyroid hormone for goiters (enlarged thyroid glands) or small, nonfunctioning thyroid glands (caused by viral infection). There is an equally large number who take it for a syndrome called hypometabolic state, which resembles thyroid deficiency and yields symptoms like dry hair, dry skin, fatigue, inability to concentrate, muscle weakness, menstrual abnormalities, fluid retention, easy weight gain, and slow weight loss. In these cases, however, the thyroid tests are normal.

I think there's a good chance that the gradual ten-to-fifteen-pound weight gain that comes with aging in women is a function of thyroid slowdown. Weight gain by itself is not a good reason to take it, but when there are other symptoms—thinning hair, loss of energy—it can make a big difference. One happy coincidence is that postmenopausal estrogen replacement seems to counteract most of these problems; one theory is that it stimulates the thyroid gland.

Even though most underburners don't have a true thyroid deficiency, the thyroid hormone plays an important role in the weight loss process. T_3 seems to assist fat breakdown, and understanding how it works can perhaps unlock one of the most puzzling and frustrating puzzles of weight loss—the plateau. A plateau is the point in your diet when, with no change in eating habits, you stop losing weight. Efforts to reduce calories further—to hardship levels—make for a sluggish, temporary resumption but also a lot of misery.

In the dark ages of the "Inquisition," we used to think that plateaus meant dieters were cheating. Physicians used to tell them it was possible they ate fattening foods *without realizing it,* as if they were Haitian zombies or something. Then some clever researchers put normalweights on a diet and found that the longer the regime lasted, the more their basal metabolic rate (rate of burning energy) slowed down. They concluded that this slowdown was the body's way of protecting its fat. The body does not see fat as a bad thing. In fact, it zealously guards it, records a set-point weight, and will fight to the finish to defend that set point. When the body gets over the shock of the initial water loss, it begins fighting back. And the sneaky way it fights back is by lowering the basal metabolic rate so you don't burn as much fat. It does so by means of a drop in T_3! This, in turn, causes:

1. Slower weight loss
2. Sensitivity to cold
3. Dry skin
4. Hair loss
5. Fluid retention

This is the thyroid deficiency of obesity. It's not a primary deficiency but an adaptive mechanism of the body to ward off starvation. Normalweights usually don't experience this "Adaptive Thyroid Response" because they don't have too much weight to lose, and by the time their body catches on to what they're doing, the diet is over. But the poor underburner, with twenty-plus pounds to lose, feels the body's full might.

You can counteract this mechanism somewhat with small amounts of a drug called Cytomel, a commercial form of T_3. A dosage of 15 micrograms—three-fifths of a grain—seems to restore fat-burning function and correct the various symptoms. In lengthy diets, doses might have to be increased.

Why, then, doesn't everyone take Cytomel to speed up weight loss? Some experts believe that the Cytomel loss is only water and protein, not fat. They might be right about the water and protein, but I think you lose fat, too. When I give Cytomel to dieters, I increase the protein content of their diet by about six grams. And I don't find water loss a problem; "dry dieters" lose weight better.

There *are* a few problems with T_3. One is that the people who need it the most are the ones most sensitive to its effects as a stimulant. T_3, as I've said, is the speedy kid on the block, and he likes to stir up the heart along with the fat cells. T_3 can cause an increased heart rate and palpitations (skipped beats). Most unpleasant. I've never seen it raise blood pressure in small doses, but theoretically it could.

It depends on the individual. Many people, females in particular, have an anatomic defect of the heart valve called "mitral valve prolapse," which makes them prime candidates for thyroid hormone oversensitivity. Also, dieting sets up a low-potassium state that makes the heart more sensitive to any stimulation. Women on diuretics for high blood pressure (often caused by obesity) should only take thyroid under close medical supervision.

The most serious problem with Cytomel has been abuse by those diet doctors who've given the profession its reputation as the sleaziest branch of medicine. These so-called doctors start patients with normal thyroid function on large doses at the beginning of a diet, and increase those doses even when patients complain of shortness of breath and a racing pulse. I got a call once from the Ethics Committee of the local medical society. They'd just received a letter from a woman who had ended up in an emergency room because her heart rate was 160 beats per minute (normal is below 90). A diet doctor had placed her on a large dose of Cytomel, and every time she had complained to him that she didn't feel well, he upped the dose. The Ethics Committee wanted to know if this was standard procedure in diet medicine. I don't need to tell you what I told them. I felt like organizing a lynching party.

Remember, Cytomel should only be used *prudently* in *carefully supervised* dieting, when you have *exhausted all other possibilities*.

Until the last few years, there weren't many other good treatments for adaptive thyroid deficiency, but I'm glad to report I've found something better than Cytomel. The new remedy:

1. Is safe
2. Is available to at least 85 per cent of dieters
3. Is inexpensive
4. Assures more fat loss than muscle loss (it actually saves muscle)

5. Makes you feel good
6. Decreases appetite

If you haven't already guessed it, the remedy is *EXERCISE!*

The only problem is that most underburners would rather take a pill than move. So it takes a lot of persuasion and promises to get them to overcome their inertia. But if that obstacle can be surmounted, there's no need for thyroid replacement to get out of a plateau.

Controlling Physical Activity

One of the underburner's basic problems is his body's inability to raise its resting metabolic rate to compensate for too many calories. That's why he can't maintain his weight even with a *modest* increase in what he eats. Since nature has not done this automatically, he must find a way to do it himself. But how?

Physical activity. It's left to the underburner to supply what Nature has unkindly left out of his system. Unfortunately Nature has also given the underburner a body type (endomorphic) and a basic personality (placid) that makes physical activity more of a challenge than for others.

Most people who conduct exercise classes are thin normalweights. At one time in their lives, they might have been normal-weight normalweights and thought they were fat. That's why they can tell you, in all seriousness, that once they were fat and look what exercise accomplished. These people never had the stumpy, square, knock-kneed, lateral look of real underburners. They were put together differently, and their bodies responded differently to exercise.

Every year at the camp where I'm a consultant, I try to explain to the slim, trim, neatly-put-together counselors that they're not working with campers built like they are. And every year the counselors lead the kids a bit too enthusiastically into vigorous exercise. So the first two weeks of camp, there's a run on ace bandages, and the infirmary starts to look like the student recreation center. The counselors aren't bad people; they just don't understand that underburners are not fat normalweights.

Different kinds of exercises do different things for the body. Calisthenics and slimnastics burn available calories and create flexibility and muscle tone. Tennis and other "spurt" sports burn calories but also increase coordination and stamina. Weight lifting builds muscle mass and promotes muscle endurance. Stationary bike riding and rowing help increase muscle strength in the extremities and are valuable for cardiovascular fitness.

But while muscle flexibility, strength, endurance, cardiovascular fitness, and coordination are all very important, I still feel that the major function of exercise in the dieting underburner is to *burn fat* and *raise resting metabolic rate.* Those needs are met by *aerobic* exercises: swimming, biking, walking, and running. Running burns more calories than any other exercise, but most underburners, with their flabby, poorly aligned ligaments and smaller muscle mass, suffer a lot of traumas— shin splints, twisted ankles, strained knees, and so on. If you're young and tough enough, however, by all means have a shot. (Make sure to have a checkup first.) That leaves three practical, fairly safe aerobic activities—swimming, biking, and walking.

Most of my patients love to swim and do water exercises, and that immediately makes me suspicious. What's more, I know a lot of chubby swimmers. The value of aerobic exercise is not just in the total movement that sends blood to all parts of your body and makes your heart beat faster, but in the work you have to do to achieve that movement. When a 190-pound man walks or runs, he's moving that 190 pounds every step of the way. When he swims, the water is making him weightless, so he's losing the advantage of his weight. Of course, he's still fighting the resistance of the water as he swims, but his actual work load is less. The same is true of biking, where the wheel does most of the work.

I don't want to put you off swimming or biking. They're fun, and they do increase your cardiovascular fitness; but in the final analysis, the exercise that gives you the most work at the least risk is walking.

Walking is good for every part of your body. For twenty minutes, you burn available calories. After that, you begin to use fat as fuel. Once fat burning is initiated, the basic metabolic rate goes up for the rest of your walk, and can stay up for several hours after you stop. I can feel this happen in the winter. When I start out, I'm cold down to my fingers. After twenty minutes, I actually feel the tips getting warmer. I know I have defeated (if only for a few hours) my sleepy metabolism.

Every time underburners eat a little bit more food than their energy-efficient bodies need, they store the excess as fat. So there probably isn't a day that goes by in which they don't store a little fat, driving their weight ever upward. But if they can burn that little bit off every day, they have a good chance of keeping their weight level—even if they don't lose. That's a victory, of sorts.

I tested my walking program on the underburner I knew most intimately—me. For one year, when I was peppy or tired, healthy or sick, in heat or cold, rain or shine. I walked my forty minutes four times a week. I did not diet; I just walked. I never went over my forty minutes either, since I didn't want my body to expect too much in the future. At the end of the year, this is what I noticed:

1. I was more physically fit and had better endurance. (I no longer dreaded climbing stairs or racing to catch a plane.)
2. I looked better. My complexion had a lovely glow.
3. My proportions were better. My hips had been trimmed considerably.
4. I had not gained any weight. For the first time in my life, my weight had stayed the same, with no change in my usual twenty-five-pound-gain-a-year eating habits.

Then I discovered even more advantages. It started when I couldn't figure out what to do with a patient who'd stopped losing weight a mere twelve pounds into her diet. We tried all the traditional tricks: a low-carbohydrate diet to see if she was holding water, and a sharp drop in calories to see if she was eating too much. So I asked her to walk forty minutes four times a week. She insisted that she *was* exercising—playing tennis, walking stairs, and so on—but I said, "Listen, one week can't kill you. If it doesn't work, your next visit's free." I didn't lose money on the deal. A week later, her craving for carbohydrates had diminished and her weight loss was back on schedule.

Walking alone helps burn calories and perhaps limits weight gain. Diet alone can be an effective way to lose weight, but the loss is unpredictable and often held up by fluid retention or metabolic changes. But if you diet and walk, you both cut calories and raise your basal metabolic rate. That guarantees a good, steady weight loss. And no other exercise does it as easily.

Unfortunately, walking is not glamorous (you won't see celebrities writing books about it), and if you're out of shape, it's hard work. But it's just forty minutes four times a week, an infinitesimal amount of time for the benefits you get. And you don't have to speed walk; a steady pace of 2.5 to 3 miles an hour does the job. Sustained slow exercise burns fat more effectively than intense fast exercise, which tends to break down your muscles.

I'm so convinced that walking is essential to a successful diet that I'm tempted to have my receptionist ask all new patients if they're willing to do it before they come in. And if they say no, I'm tempted to send them elsewhere. That's not fair, I know, but in this business, who needs more grief?

Controlling Volume

Gastric Bypass

Morbid obesity is defined as obesity so severe that it interferes with work, play, and personal hygiene. More objectively, it's when a body exceeds its ideal weight by more than one hundred pounds. The morbidly obese person has tried every conceivable weight-loss plan and has emerged heavier and more frustrated than ever. The answer is clearly not medical; perhaps, someone once ventured, it's surgical.

One early surgical procedure was stomach-stapling. Sounds like something out of *Friday the 13th,* right? Doctors observed, in normal-weights, that if a large portion of their stomach was removed (to control severe ulcer disease), they couldn't consume enough calories to maintain their weight. What a plus that would be for underburners! Rather than *removing* the stomach (a permanent step), surgeons decided merely to alter its volume by stapling two-thirds of it closed but allowing a small opening for passage of food. What you ate went through the normal digestive process, but if you ate too much, you vomited. Many people still had to go on a calorie-restricted program to lose all their weight; but with their smaller stomachs, interestingly enough, they reported less preoccupation with food and fewer cravings.

For a while I was excited about gastric stapling. It would limit how much food you could eat, cause you to fill up faster, and make it impossible to eat enough to remain fat. At least, that was my thinking before I met the three big girls.

I first saw Donna in 1977. She was thirty-nine years old and had by that time had her uterus, ovaries, gallbladder, and thyroid removed. In fact, there was very little left of her except 272 pounds of adipose tissue —fat. Her diets had ranged from the sensible to the ludicrous to the dangerous.

I placed her on a very low calorie diet, and she reduced to 188 pounds. Very good. Then she stopped coming to the office and returned in a panic three months later, having binged and gained twenty-five pounds. Her impulsive eating pattern and rapid weight gain forced me to hospitalize her to try to protect a portion of her loss. In the hospital, she lost twenty pounds and then disappeared from treatment after discharge.

She returned in 1981, stating she'd had a stomach stapling in December of 1979 and had lost approximately ninety pounds. Then, gradually, she found she could eat more and more. X rays revealed that the staple hadn't broken, but for some reason what was left of her stomach could expand to whatever size it needed to be. On her last visit, she weighed 270 and was going to a Naturopath for a high colonic (a weekly enema) and a liver flush (which was supposed to get rid of the toxins). I wonder what she'll try next.

Millie was forty-nine years old, five-foot-three, 250 pounds, and wanted a gastric stapling. A psychiatrist had declared her a good candidate for the operation, and I was supposed to supervise her postoperative feeding. She had no teeth, but she assured me she could eat anything and was ready to follow a diet after surgery. She lost thirty pounds in the hospital. When I went in to see her—she still had tubes sticking out—I instructed her on what she could eat when she got home.

Five days after discharge, Millie phoned to say she was vomiting all the food on her diet. Two weeks later, she phoned again, saying she couldn't tolerate meat because she couldn't chew. We supplied a soft, low-calorie diet of eggs, skim milk, cottage cheese, vegetables, and some strained fruit. She phoned and said she couldn't follow that diet either and was eating whatever she made for her family, but less. She then informed me that after four P.M., ice cream was the only food she could keep down. Millie was worried she would die of malnutrition. I don't have to tell you what happened to her weight.

Kitty was forty years old, five-foot-three, and 276 pounds. A surgeon told her that gastric stapling was the answer to all her problems. He never mentioned the risks or told her she'd have to change her eating habits. The surgery was performed and she had every complication known to man: hemorrhage, shock, rupture, infection, and even a blood clot in the lung. When she was finally released from the hospital two months later, she had lost about forty pounds.

I saw her a year after the surgery and her weight was back to 275. She skipped meals, refused to keep food records, and claimed that her income was such that she couldn't possibly follow a diet (even though we worked out a diet that would accommodate her budget). Her food diary disclosed that she was eating jelly donuts, pizzas, soup, nuts. She said she could eat as much as she did before her operation.

I am currently treating about a quarter of a million dollars' worth of surgical failures. These carefully screened patients had experienced long, painful postoperative recovery ("The worst pain I ever felt," said one), lost perhaps fifty of their excess 150 pounds during the trauma of surgery, and went on to develop an aversion for every low-calorie food. They ate only two ounces of food at a time, but they ate continuously— always full but still hungry.

No major procedure has been more worthless for treating female underburners than decreasing the size of their stomachs. I must add, however, that the few males I saw with stomach-staplings did much better in the weight loss and maintenance departments. It's probably because they tend to eat much larger quantities and less often.

Changing the size of a stomach assumes that appetite is controlled by volume alone and not by other changes in brain chemistry. Evidently, a full stomach does not mean your brain will stop saying "Feed Me." For the rest of us, that means that you can fill your stomach with diet soda, water, and bulky, low-calorie food and still be hungry, even if you're unable to eat.

The new gastric bubble—a plastic bubble inserted in the stomach through a tube, inflated, kept in place for several months and then withdrawn—will be the stomach-stapling of the future. It's a relatively safe, nontraumatic procedure, and initial reports indicate that it actually suppresses appetite and hunger. Both come back, however, when the tube is removed, a mere three months later.

Oddly enough, the gastric bubble has been approved for people with as little as 20 percent excess body fat, so you might see normalweights walking around with them in a couple of years.

Controlling Absorption

Intestinal Bypass

I have argued that severe, long-term dieting is inhumane. Some of my colleagues agree with me, and the medical profession does have its share of committed *healers*. The most humane of that group are the surgeons, who devised a procedure for underburners to eat pretty much what they wanted and still lose weight. It was a simple operation that involved bypassing a segment of the small intestine so that only 30 percent of the food you ate would actually be absorbed. The rest would be excreted.

The operation led to complications, including dehydration, liver failure, kidney stones, kidney failure, malnutrition, and bone disease. Less dangerous but equally annoying side effects were continual diarrhea and a foul-smelling gas that required many of the patients to carry spray deodorants. Some of these were due to poor surgical techniques, others were from an inadequate grasp of the procedure itself. The original surgeons *should* have realized that along with loss of calories goes loss of vitamins, minerals, and fluids.

Everybody was ecstatically happy before the appearance of complications. But the disasters were so numerous that intestinal bypasses have been virtually discontinued; many of the original patients have been reconnected.

Oddly enough, the survivors swear that eating all they wanted for a while was worth the trauma.

Starch Inhibitors and Blockers

A much safer way to stop your body from absorbing calories was the use of so-called starch blockers. The drug (or more correctly, the food) was a legume protein concentrate (extracted from the northern white bean) that was supposed to inhibit alpha-amylase, the enzyme in the pancreas that digests starch. So you could theoretically pig out on starches and not gain a pound. More realistically, it means that successful dieting wouldn't have to be so tough. Just think: baked potatoes, rice, and pasta primavera could slide through the intestine with hardly a calorie absorbed.

Imagine my excitement when I heard about them from several West Coast investigators, who claimed to have used them successfully on four hundred subjects. I was my first patient. I took those little antistarch pills and I swear I lost some weight without curtailing my food intake. However, I also had strange pains in the area of my pancreas. I guess everyone who belted down starch blockers had the same weird pain, because in a two-week period, the nation's emergency rooms were flooded with (you guessed it) gassy underburners. In no time, the Food and Drug Administration stepped in and banned the pills altogether.

The FDA said that any substance advertised as blocking a pancreatic enzyme would have to be labeled a *drug* and not a *food.* That meant it would have to go through the usual years and years of testing before it could be returned to the market. As far as I know, starch blockers are dead. And I think that's too bad. They might have been dangerous, in the long run, but they were still *the right idea,* and I wish someone had thought to experiment and develop them. Apart from intestinal bypasses, no other treatment for obesity had addressed itself to the problem of absorption.

Controlling the Fat Cell

Liposuction

Scientists have spent a lot of time studying appetite, metabolism, and behavior but have ignored the *thing itself,* the wily and energy-rich fat cell. If only the poor underburners who overproduce fat cells could donate them to society, then they'd be happy (and thin) and we'd all have a near-permanent source of fuel.

Seriously, why not just remove excess fat? Cut it off. We remove excess skin and hair, and if someone had two stomachs, I'm sure we'd remove one of them. Why not fat? Diet and exercise are such indirect ways of dealing with the problem. True, I've read horror stories about movie stars in the 1920s and 1930s getting "defatted" and being left with horrible scars and infections. A few even died. But things should be different today.

They are.

Lucy was a fifty-five-year-old, five-foot-five female and a former Weight Watchers lecturer. She'd been fired because she couldn't maintain a goal weight of 142 pounds that the organization had set for her.

She had lost about 100 pounds in one year and presently weighed 147. I figured that at age twenty-five, her set-point weight had been 140, so, allowing for age and increased fat-cell mass, her present goal weight should have been 160.

But Lucy was starved, badgered, and threatened with job loss if her weight got any higher than 147. She looked terrible: The upper half of her body was skeletal, but her hips, legs, and thighs were filled with lumpy, unsightly fat that refused, with all her starvation and exercise, to budge. As much as she tried, she couldn't keep her weight down to 147. Whenever her daily caloric intake exceeded 1,000, her weight climbed to 157.

We know now what made the fat on certain parts of her body so resistant to weight loss. In females, the typical body build is pear-shaped, and this area of fat on the hips and thighs (saddlebag fat) is the *stable* fat, or the fat that's genetically placed and hormonally protected. It's almost impossible to lose by conventional methods. (As I mentioned in the pregnancy chapter, stable fat in women is only available for use in the last three months of pregnancy and during lactation; in men, stable fat is in the abdomen and available only in case of extreme exercise and starvation.) So a woman could starve herself, deplete her muscle mass, and still not get rid of that saddlebag fat.

What could you do for Lucy, short of cutting her fat out? That's it! Cut her fat out. Plastic surgeons were starting to do a procedure called *liposuctioning,* or suction lipectomy, for fat distribution that created figure problems in young women.

The procedure is quite simple. The surgeon inserts a curette (a spoon-shaped surgical instrument) through a very small incision into the offending fat, switches on the suction, and, lo and behold, fat in the bottle and not in the thigh. Why not use this technique to suck out my patient's ugly, immovable fat, lower her total fat-cell number, reduce her weight, perhaps lower her set point, correct her figure problems, save her job, and make everyone happy?

I called several plastic surgeons and, one by one, they refused. Some were generously willing to do a cosmetic reconstruction on the tops of her legs at a cost of three to four thousand a leg. Although I explained that cosmetics were not the problem—that survival and a job were at stake—those boys were adamant.

Why did the plastic surgeons refuse to do suction lipectomy on my patient? Because they were afraid they wouldn't get perfect results.

Their guidelines for doing this procedure recommend that candidates for liposuction have no medical problems, good skin tone, and, most important, not be obese. It didn't matter that they could probably do a lot of good using liposuction in the area of obesity.

I told them: "Fat people who want liposuction are motivated by a different set of desires than thin people, and *perfect contour* isn't one of them. They don't dream about bikinis or see themselves in sexy love scenes. A little loose skin or a tiny scar wouldn't send them into a tizzy. They'd just be happy to get rid of a few million fat cells. They'd like the feel of wearing fitted clothes without being self-conscious. Have you ever looked at a lumpy, obese leg? Don't you think these people would be satisfied with having a smooth obese leg, particularly if it meant those lumps might never come back again?"

Plastic surgeons tend not to hear what they don't want to hear.

I'm glad to say we finally found someone willing to do my patient's liposuction, but it wasn't a plastic surgeon. It was a cosmetic surgeon, part of a new group of loosely tied-together specialties that include Ear, Nose, and Throat; Dermatology; General Surgery; and Gynecology. These men and women, all of them trained in liposurgery, seem less concerned about perfect cosmetics and more willing to help underburners get rid of stubborn fat.

I think this *might* be the operation of the future for obesity—safer than bypassing intestines and less complicated than stapling stomachs. It would decrease the number of fat cells and, thus, make it impossible for them to reopen. In fact, liposuction is so exciting that I persuaded my husband, a gynecologist, to learn the technique. In the future, we'll be able to evaluate the results together.

Understand, it's a mistake to think that we can totally de-fat a person, because only about 2,000 cc of fat can be removed at any one time. That's about four or five pounds, hardly the difference between fat and thin. But remember, fat itself is quite light (recall how it rises to the top of soup), so four or five pounds make up a surprising volume. Moreover, it is a *crucial* four or five pounds—it's in the specific area of your biggest and most unsightly fat collection. So your face will stay full while your hips (or stomach or chin) get thin.

There's another twist. The time to remove fat cells is not in their fully expanded state, but when they're small. Every obese person is capable of one or two major weight losses in a lifetime, and it's toward the end of such a loss that the liposuction procedure should be performed on areas that still have bulges. In the pears (the bottom-heavy folks), that would be the hips, upper thighs and abdomen; in the ice-cream cones (the top-heavy folks), it might be the back and upper arms. At that point in the diet, the removal of four or five pounds would include both open and closed fat cells. Those small, closed fat cells have the potential to reopen again and can represent *20 to 30 pounds.* That's an incredible amount of fat for so little trauma.

Complications from liposuction are minimal in well-trained hands. The most annoying and distressing include waviness, dents (from removing too much fat), bruising, hematomas (collections of blood under the skin), and soreness. The worst complications—blood clots, infections, excessive bleeding, and the hazards of anesthesia (general, low spinal, or local)—are potentially present in all surgical procedures.

One complication that I think can be controlled is the fatigue a lot of patients experience. This is probably caused by blood loss, which in inexperienced hands can be significant. Fat has a very rich blood supply —several miles of capillaries for every pound. But I think part of the fatigue is also due to potassium loss. Fat cells have a lot of potassium. I see fatigue with gradual fat loss all the time, so it should be even more significant in rapid weight loss. After all, these cells maintain a comfortable equilibrium with the rest of the body, and their removal is bound to disturb that.

Another problem I've seen is psychological: the amount of fat removed has been so insignificant, and the price so astronomically high (as in most plastic-surgery procedures), that the patients get justifiably depressed. This will change, I hope, as surgeons learn more about the operation and the prices come down.

Liposuction surgery is not for women alone. Male underburners (and a few normalweights) now have a chance to lose embarrassing bosoms, fat bellies, and sloppy love handles. A testimony to the safety and simplicity of this surgery in men is that many doctors who perform the procedure have had it done on themselves!

My only reservation about liposuction is that there's a chance the body, sensing the loss of all those fat cells, could somehow manufacture lots of new ones. At this writing, there's no evidence that will happen, but this is, admittedly, early in the game. And where protecting fat is concerned, I wouldn't put anything past the human body.

Obesity remains a wide open field. Got a theory? Sound crazy? It

doesn't matter. What could be crazier than having your intestines dis-
connected, chewing on frog skin, or going on some weird diet that
might screw up your heart rhythm? Maybe the Scandinavians had the
best diet plan—"The Somnolent Diet." On it, you'd sleep for a month
and get up only to drink some water or go to the bathroom. Then back
to bed. Voilà! Four weeks later you'd wake up thin (or thinner). If you
woke up, that is.

    Magic.

Chapter 16

FAT WARS

The Ultimate Defense

Whenever I paint the grim metabolic picture for underburners, some people get angry. "It's all very well to tell us about our bodies," they say. "But what do we *do* about them? What's the ultimate solution?"

Frankly, I don't think there is one. Yet. Other books about weight loss have ultimate solutions, but if they were so ultimate, you wouldn't be reading this one. The dieting establishment says that the solution is *self-control:* Learn to live in a semistarvation state and get a reasonable amount of exercise (four hours a day might do it, ha-ha).

In my last book, I made an inflammatory statement: "Never eat sugar or flour again." Unrealistic. Depressing. A downer. Okay, I can play the feel-good game. If you want magic wands and yellow brick roads and emerald cities, hang onto your stomach and follow me over the rainbow.

Final Solution #1: Take diet pills forever. If you have to live starved, get chemical help. You can always find a semiretired doctor who's sick of all the medical hypocrisy and will give you some pills. He might die, however, or be exposed by a zealous reporter.

Final Solution #2: Keep smoking. It will kill your appetite, lower your set point, and raise your basal metabolic rate. It will kill you, too, but hell—you'll die thin!

Final Solution #3: Become a wet nurse. Prolactin, the hormone that stimulates milk production, also burns fat. It's a greater service than donating blood. And all those beautiful, hungry babies!

Final Solution #4: Get a suction lipectomy. Find a doctor who'll take your money and suck those fat cells out of your thighs, hips, stomach, buttocks, and chin. Tell him to keep sucking, never stop sucking.

Final Solution #5: Get an intestinal bypass. It's like Russian roulette, of course, but hey, live fast, die young. You'll probably have liver failure, kidney stones, and massive vitamin deficiencies in a couple of years—and they will kill you, eventually—but until then, *live to eat.*

Final Solution #6: Get a bubble. This balloon-like gadget is easily passed into the stomach and inflated. It makes it almost impossible to eat—you feel too full. What a shame it's got to come out in only three months. But you've learned to eat correctly, right? At least correctly with a balloon in your stomach. So don't show up to have it out. Who'll know the difference?

The above suggestions are a joke, of course. But they *are* solutions—although radical, expensive, and often lethal. As tired, glum, and unmagical as it sounds to say, "Eat less, move more," it's still the best advice we have.

What can science do for underburners?

Give them the right to eat a reasonable amount of food without getting fat. Since that is, at the moment, impossible, the answer will be a pill to make all men and women metabolically equal. The pill could be named "Fat Wars," after the Reagan "Star Wars" Strategic Defense Initiative. Like "Star Wars," "Fat Wars" will keep the missiles from landing on our cities—or, in this case, the fat molecules from landing in our cells. That's it, folks: the ultimate defense.

I doubt the Administration will ever cough up the kind of funds for "Fat Wars" that they've talked about for "Star Wars." But it's something to dream about as you stare into the night sky, exhausted from worrying about how much you weigh, what you can eat before bedtime, what you'll have for breakfast, and on and on.

In the meantime, I hope this book will assist you in separating the diets that can help you from the ones that will just leave you frustrated —or, worse yet, endanger your health. The more you know about your own body and the more realistic you are about your chances of losing and maintaining weight, the better those chances become. In dieting, as in most areas, knowledge is power, and I trust that I've given you lots of food for thought. Those are calories you really ought to be storing.

APPENDIX A

Fifty Best Diet Foods

Diets go in and out of fashion, but diet food is forever. No matter what the fad or where it's centered—Scarsdale, Beverly Hills, or Poughkeepsie—a grapefruit in the morning gets you off to a great start. It's low in calories, high in nutrients, and readily available. Here, then, is an alphabetical listing, by food types, of the 50 Best Foods for Dieters.

If you wish to substitute for any of the foods on your diet, you'd do well to choose one from the same category in this list.

Meat, Fish, Fowl:

Chicken, white meat. The most palatable, versatile, and popular protein. 1/2 breast is 160 calories.

Cornish Hen. Underutilized, lowfat fowl. 1/2 whole is 230 calories.

Fish, fatty (salmon and swordfish). Considered healthier in spite of extra calories because they contain oils that lower cholesterol. One serving three ounces 170–180 calories.

Fish, nonfat. King of the low-calorie proteins, but not as well liked by teenagers as chicken. One serving is 70–90 calories.

Fish, water-packed tuna. This deserves its own listing, because surely no diet in this country could survive without it. One small can is 127 calories.

Hamburger, lean (less than 17% fat). Surprise: Lean beef actually does not have that many more calories than the high-fat fishes, but of course the fat is saturated. (And it is rarely available commercially with this little fat.) Surprise: Nutrient is 480 mg of potassium. One serving is 140–160 calories.

Seafood (crabmeat, lobster, shrimp). Cholesterol content is less than half that of eggs but has received bad press lately. Not common enough component of diet to worry about. Use as luxury food. One serving is 90–100 calories.

Tenderloin. The ideal restaurant treat food when you want to pamper yourself without too much damage. (Don't worry: Few places can ruin it.) One serving is 187 calories.

Turkey, white meat. Now a practical diet food, since turkey breasts are readily available. You can roast one on Sunday night, and still be eating it the following Friday. One serving is 180 calories.

Dairy Products:

The egg. No doubt cholesterol content is a problem, but for most women and men without heart disease, it's an economical and readily available food. Consider using two pure protein whites for one yolk. One egg is 80 calories and is loaded with vitamin A.

Cottage cheese, low-fat, creamed. Easy to digest, unless you are lactose intolerant. Though it tends to behave more like a carbohydrate in the body, it is a good source of protein for the vegetarian or the person who hates to chew. One cup is 200 calories.

Milk, skim. Good low-calorie snack that does not stimulate appetite. Particularly good before bedtime, since a high level of tryptophan stimulates sleep. One 8-ounce glass is 81 calories.

Yogurt, plain. I hear they've found Russian yogurt-eating peasants living to be over one hundred years old. Not to be outdone, Americans have developed a taste for it. Good high-protein, low-fat food that can be used as a meal, a dessert, or an appetizer. One cup is 122 calories and is rich in potassium, not to mention calcium.

Grains:

Bagel. This is the food most asked for by my dieters. ("When can I have a half a bagel on Sunday morning?") Great as filler, a half goes a long way. Available now in high-fiber varieties, like whole wheat and rye. One bagel is 155 calories.

Bread, whole wheat. Whenever bread enters a diet, it should be whole wheat because of the fiber. As dieting progresses it can be substituted for a fruit, though underburners must be careful with this addition early in the diet. One slice is 60 calories.

Cereal, regular (boxed). This is my favorite cheat food, since I can eat a whole cup and not destroy a diet. Of course there is a wide range in calories, but if you avoid the ones with added sugar, there should be no problems. One cup is anywhere from 50 to 110 calories.

Cereal, whole grain. This food is once again becoming popular, particularly oatmeal and oat bran (it may lower cholesterol). In addition, it generally has no caloric additives like the cold cereals. One cup cooked is 131 calories.

Melba toast. This is the kind in the package and was the only bread concession I made on my original Core Diet. It stays here for sentimental purposes. One piece is 16 calories.

Pita bread. The new fun bread that gives you the illusion of getting more for your calories. One-half of a small one could be considered a diet portion. Makes a great receptacle for tuna fish. One small pita is 60 calories.

Rice, brown. You must cook this longer than white rice, but high fiber content makes it worth the trouble. One cup is 190 calories.

Rice, white. Not as good for you as brown rice but more available in those important places we like to eat, like Chinese restaurants! (Though I'm told brown rice is appearing there too.) One cup is 185 calories.

Condiments:

Garlic. Reported to have some effect in lowering blood fats. In addition, jazzes up bland diet. Most important, where can you get such a calorie bargain? One bulb is 2 calories.

Vinegar. Another flavor enhancer, good for everyone except the mold-allergy sufferers (who can use lemon juice at 5 calories a tablespoon). Available now with many different bases and flavors. One tablespoon is 2 calories.

Fruits:

Apple. A wonderful, filling, fiber-rich fruit. It might just keep the doctor away. One apple is 90–100 calories.

Banana. A banana makes everyone feel like they are not dieting; it's that little bit of fat that does it. Still, it is not a *fattening* fruit, and it is rich in potassium. One banana is 130 calories.

Berries. These have a double advantage: They can be put on things like cereal or low-calorie Jell-O (even other fruits) or enjoyed one by one. One cup of the more popular ones is 85–90 calories.

Grapefruit. This is not the magical fruit it is supposed to be: It does not burn fat. It is just a good, filling, available, economical, easy-to-digest fruit. One whole is 80 calories.

Melon (cantaloupe, watermelon). These are more seasonal diet foods, but their popularity makes it important to include them. They are both rich in vitamin A, and watermelon is no more fattening than bananas. ½ cantaloupe is 60 calories. One 1-inch thick slice of watermelon is 115 calories.

Orange. The juice is overrated, but the whole fruit is still "sunshine." It's loaded with vitamins A and C, and peeling it is good exercise. One orange is 65–70 calories.

Pineapple. Since Hawaii became our fiftieth state, the pineapple has been growing in popularity. Better shipping methods are getting the fruit here in more edible condition. Forget the myth that pineapples contain a fat-digesting enzyme (not true)—just appreciate the good taste and filling capacity. Although canning alters taste and consistency, it is not unpleasant. ¼ whole is 90 calories.

Pear. This old standby when you are sick of apples and oranges is so versatile and available it must be included on this list. One pear is 120 calories.

Raisins. I personally do not like dried fruits on a diet: They're too sugar concentrated. But life without raisins would be hard to face. Sprinkled on hot or cold cereal, or just munched slowly, these potassium- and iron-rich morsels can make you very happy. One tablespoon is 60 calories.

Vegetables:

If you don't like vegetables, you might as well give up the idea of dieting. These are the filler and the backbone of a diet, taking the place of the pure starches and fats that you give up. What's more, they provide a varied and rich supply of vitamins and minerals. (The yellow vegetables are rich in beta-carotene, which may reduce the risk of certain cancers; the leafy green vegetables are rich in the B vitamins). You should learn to eat them without the addition of a lot of fat. (If you can't eat corn without butter, then you really don't like the taste of corn.)

Broccoli. One cup is 40 calories.
Brussel sprouts. One cup is 50 calories.
Carrots. One is 30 calories; one cup is 45 calories.
Cauliflower. One cup is 27 calories.
Corn. Eat fresh only. One ear is 100 calories.
Cucumbers (and dill pickles, too). One is 14 calories.
Legumes (meat substitute only). One cup (raw) is 400 calories.
Lettuce. One head is 60 calories.
Mushrooms. One cup is 25 calories.
Onion. One is 40 calories.
Peppers. One green is 15 calories; one red is 20.
Potato, white. Acts like a sugar after it's ingested and can stimu-
      late the appetite. One is 120 calories.
Spinach. One cup cooked is 40 calories.
String beans. One cup is 30 calories.
Summer squash. One cup is 30 calories.
Tomato. One is 35 calories.
Turnip (my favorite filler vegetable). One cup is 35 calories.

You see what calorie bargains most of the vegetables are. Even Underburners could stay reasonably close to their set-point weight if they used them as filler for a normal diet.

A simple daily diet formula for the Underburner would be:

Two proteins
One and one-half grains or starch
Three fruits
Six vegetables (not including potato)
One dairy product
Vitamins
One tablespoon of unprocessed bran
6 eight-ounce glasses of water

APPENDIX B

Jazzing Up Your Diet

I used to think that diets should be boring. The plainer the food, the more successful the diet, I thought. The notion of spending hours in the kitchen *is* counterproductive, especially since underburners overrespond to tempting food cues. But now I see the need for variety when you're cutting your calories so low. The catch is that it's got to be variety *at the lowest cost in time and calories.*

One night I was dining in a fancy French restaurant and was, as usual, on a diet. "No sauces," I told the horrified waiter.

"But, madam," he said, "the chef will be upset. His sauces are superb. The food will taste ordinary without them."

I wanted to remind him that fresh, well-cooked, skillfully seasoned food does not taste "ordinary," but I held my tongue. The concerned chef, however, came out of the kitchen to see why I'd made my request, and, when he found out about my diet, assured me he could make a coulis (a purée of vegetables) that would be both low calorie and delicious. I agreed, but only if it could be served on the side. (I didn't trust him.)

My entrée that night was lamb medallions, lean and juicy. They were delicious plain, but with the addition of a red pepper purée sauce, they were ethereal. Suddenly, the possibilities seemed limitless.

SWEET RED PEPPER SAUCE

The beauty of this sauce is its simplicity and delicate taste. It is marvelous on lamb and chicken.

2 sweet red peppers, sliced
1 teaspoon of corn oil

Sauté peppers over low heat until soft. Purée.

PIMENTO SAUCE

A variation of the above sauce uses bottled pimento. This has a little more snap in it and tastes great over asparagus or broccoli, as well as a bland cut of meat like tenderloin.

1 jar of pimentoes
1 teaspoon corn oil
1 tablespoon vinegar

Purée.

The summer tomato is a wonderful vegetable and has saved many diets from disaster. But it's still not used to its fullest potential. Most winter tomatoes are dismal, but a switch to the canned plum variety can be made with surprisingly little sacrifice in taste.

TOMATO SAUCE #1

2 medium-size tomatoes, peeled, chopped, but not seeded
1 teaspoon corn oil
1/2 teaspoon sugar

Sauté tomatoes in oil, add sugar, and cook over low heat seven minutes. Use over green vegetables, beef, or nonoily fish. A delicious variation of this is to sauté one thinly sliced onion with the tomatoes.

TOMATO SAUCE #2

1 large can plum tomatoes
2 tablespoons tomato paste
1 packet artificial sugar
1/2 teaspoon dried basil
1 large fresh tomato, chopped, with skin

Combine first three ingredients and simmer for 15 minutes. Purée. Add chopped fresh tomato and cook an additional five minutes.

TOMATO SAUCE #3

This sauce makes a definite Italian statement and can be served over baked meatballs, spaghetti squash, broiled eggplant, and sauteed green and red peppers. A little goes a long way. You can vary it, at little cost caloriewise, with one cup of mushrooms or one tablespoon of Parmesan or Romano cheese. For an entirely different flavor, omit the basil and add one teaspoon of cumin and one-half teaspoon of turmeric. Then it's chili time.

> *2 large cans Italian plum tomatoes*
> *1 teaspoon olive oil*
> *5 cloves garlic, minced*
> *1 teaspoon basil*
> *1/4 teaspoon oregano*
> *1 teaspoon sugar*

Simmer for 1/2 hour.

SALSA

> *2 cans stewed tomatoes*
> *2 large onions, chopped*
> *1 large green pepper, chopped*
> *One teaspoon red pepper flakes*
> *Pinch of oregano*

Cook together until vegetables are cooked.
Season to taste.
Cool and allow flavors to mellow overnight.

This is good served on vegetable salad, shredded chicken, sliced cold flank steak, and as a dip.

Most of these tomato sauces are only 20 to 30 calories a tablespoon, but they make the dieter feel like he's getting a special treat and help relieve the boredom of bland meals.

BARBECUE SAUCE

No discussion of sauces would be complete without a barbecue-sauce recipe. It's hard to imagine the amount of sugar that goes into these sauces. I was forced to use artificial sugar to get the proper taste, but purists may wish to use honey. This will add only minimally to the calories.

> *1 large can tomato sauce*
> *2 onions, chopped*
> *1 carrot, finely grated*
> *2 tablespoons Dijon-type mustard, or Hot and Sweet Mustard*
> *1 tablespoon cider vinegar*
> *1 tablespoon steak sauce*
> *4 packets Sweet 'n Low, or 2 tablespoons of honey*
> *2 or 3 dashes of Tabasco*

Simmer ingredients together for one hour. Allow flavors to mellow in refrigerator overnight. Use one tablespoon, as an accompaniment to charcoaled meats, chicken, or roasted vegetables.

MUSHROOM DUXELLES

This is something a little different. While not exactly a sauce, it's a superb flavor enhancer and has only about 20 calories a tablespoon. The final result is an intensely flavored mushroom concentrate, which can be added to scrambled eggs, tucked in the center of meatballs, or stuffed into the underside of a chicken breast.

> *1 pound of clean, firm mushrooms, chopped fine*
> *1 teaspoon margarine*

Sauté mushrooms slowly for about one half-hour or until water has been absorbed. Season to taste.

The Mock Sour Cream Sauces

Plain, unflavored yogurt is the dieter's sour cream and, if used properly, can create the illusion of richness. It is only about 127 calories an eight-ounce container, it keeps in the fridge for a long time, and a little goes a long way. Drain a little of the liquid off to give it a firmer consistency.

YOGURT CUCUMBER SAUCE (Raita)

1 8-ounce container of plain yogurt
1 large cucumber, peeled and chopped
1/4 cup fresh chopped dill, or 1 teaspoon dried dill, or
*   1 teaspoon roasted, ground cumin*

Mix together. Season to taste with salt and pepper. Allow to mellow overnight. Serve over poached salmon, chopped raw vegetables, or sliced tomatoes and onions. The same recipe, with the addition of *sliced* cucumbers and onions, becomes a side dish for barbecued chicken.

SOUTH OF THE BORDER SAUCE

1 8-ounce container of plain unflavored yogurt
1 teaspoon cumin
1 teaspoon coriander
2 chopped scallions
5 green olives, chopped

Mix together. Allow flavors to mellow. Can be used as a dip for jicama or as a topping for a taco salad, with shredded lettuce, browned lean hamburger, chopped tomatoes, and 1 ounce grated low-fat cheese.

POOR MAN'S PESTO

I have never been a pesto fan, but for those who love it, this is a surprisingly tasty low-calorie version.

1 cup plain yogurt
1 clove garlic
1 packed cup basil leaves

Purée together and serve on cooked vegetables, or rice.

Here are some other quick yogurt ideas:

3 tablespoons yogurt
1 tablespoon mustard

Mix.

Brush on swordfish and broil 10 minutes on one side.

3 tablespoons yogurt
2 teaspoons honey
1 teaspoon vanilla

Mix. Put one tablespoon over fresh fruit salad or sliced oranges.

3 tablespoons yogurt
1 teaspoon curry powder
1 tablespoon minced apple

Mix and coat two boneless, skinless chicken breasts. Bake 25 minutes in moderate oven.

Skimmed-milk creamed cottage cheese has a few more calories than yogurt (198 for an 8-ounce serving), but is also sweeter and richer. It makes a great dip mixed with horseradish and chopped onion or with cooked spinach and dried leek soup.

Diet mayonnaise, which is acceptable for fish and egg salads, also makes quick, rich-tasting sauces. 1 tablespoon of diet mayonnaise mixed with one teaspoon of mustard and a touch of tarragon creates a delightful béarnaise for beef. Add a little ketchup and chopped pickle to the same mayonnaise, and you have a deceptively rich sauce for seafood.

Low-Calorie Salad Dressings

Patients complain constantly about how terrible low-calorie salad dressings taste and are always asking me to recommend the best ones. I find the Kraft Zesty and Oil-Free and Bernstein's diet dressing acceptable, but I admit that none of them are that great. If you don't want your salad plain or with vinegar or lemon juice, they're better than nothing.

If I have time, I doctor them up with 1 teaspoon of nonfat dry milk, chopped garlic and parsley, and a pinch of artificial sweetener.

Low-calorie dressings actually make wonderful meat marinades. Since they're so pungent, they also act like a tenderizer.

MARINADE

Combine:
1/2 bottle of your favorite Italian or French dressing
2 cloves garlic, crushed

Marinate chicken or flank steak a minimum of four hours.

Broil or charcoal to desired doneness and return the meat to the marinade. The meat or chicken juices will mellow the sharpness of the dressing.

The creamier low-calorie dressings are wonderful for raw vegetable dips, either plain or mixed with low-fat cottage cheese. They have such sharp flavors that no other seasoning is needed, except for freshly ground pepper and garlic. The addition of a few anchovies or some crumbled blue cheese can make them a little more provocative.

Sometimes during the course of a long diet, all animal protein becomes repugnant. That's the time to try a sweet meat. It's easy. You just combine your meat course with your fruit. Chicken breasts baked in orange juice and garnished with orange slices are a nice change. Or try turkey breast basted with apple juice and served with an apple sauce. Apples cooked slowly with cinnamon become apple butter and are delicious over lean, center-cut roast pork. And a slightly thickened pineapple-mandarin orange sauce (one tablespoon of cornstarch is only 27 calories) spiked with soy sauce is great over meatballs. If you're getting a little tired of plain broiled fish, sample filet of sole with grapefruit sections or swordfish with raspberry purée.

The Oriental influence can give a whole new dimension to cooking. You should learn to appreciate not only the familiar soy and teriyaki sauces but also plum sauce and oyster sauce. Not to mention sesame and chili oils.

Crisp-cook 1 pound of string beans, add 2 tablespoons of soy sauce and a drop of sesame oil. Reheat carefully over moderately high heat until all the liquid has evaporated. The final result tastes fattening but isn't. Carrots and broccoli can be prepared this way also. Brush a turkey breast with a mixture of 3 parts soy sauce and 1 part honey. Roast one hour in a pan with 1 cup of orange juice. Turkey never had it so good.

If you feel my simple methods for jazzing up your diet are still too complicated, then try basting meat or fish with flavored vinegars— blueberry for chicken, raspberry for swordfish, or rice vinegar for salads. And don't forget the myriad herbs and spices in your spice rack, such as rosemary, thyme, mustard seed, the new Cajun spices, and herbs of the province.

APPENDIX C

A Guide to Common Diet-Related Signs and Symptoms

About half of the phone calls that I get in my office are inquiries about symptoms that appear during or after a diet. There is a tendency when dieting to blame everything that happens on the diet. While many symptoms are diet related, others have nothing to do with it. I have been keeping track of these phone calls for about six months and have picked out some of the most common diet-related problems people ask about. This is just a fast reference guide to help you understand what's happening.

Key:

Frequency of Occurrences   Sex most affected

   Common (C)   Female (F)

   Occasional (O)   Male (M)

   Unusual (U)

   Rare (R)

Bad breath (halitosis): Caused by the metabolic state of ketosis, in which the body burns fat more efficiently. It gives breath a heavy fruity or acidic odor. (Increased acid in the stomach that is not buffered by food can also add to unpleasant breath odor.) Use Tums to neutralize the odors and also supply you with calcium. (C,M,F)

Bruising: Black and blue marks (*ecchymosis*) often appear in women without any injury or not enough injury to merit the size of the bruise. This is a result of an increased level of circulating estrogen in the body, which somehow weakens the walls of the capillary and causes it to break under the slightest pressure. When it breaks, blood escapes, causing a bruise. Estrogen is broken down in the liver, and so is fat. When you are on a diet, the liver preferentially breaks down the fat, leaving a lot more estrogen in the bloodstream. Increased doses of vitamin C (1000 mg) toughens the walls of the capillaries so they don't rupture. (O,F)

Cold sensitivity (cold intolerance): Increased sensitivity to cold temperatures, even air conditioning. Fat insulates, and when it is lost, this insulation is lost. Fingers, toes, and even the tip of the nose can become easily chilled. Dress warmly, particularly after large winter weight loss. (C,M)

Constipation: Change in consistency and sometimes frequency of bowel movement. Decreased total food intake in addition to decreased carbohydrate intake and increased fluid loss are the causes. Addition of natural fiber and water are helpful. (C,F)

Depression: Feelings of sadness or emptiness out of proportion to any personal problem. Most dieters are unhappy about having to diet but few are genuinely depressed. The exception is premenstrually, in females where premenstrual syndrome includes depression, irritability, and weight gain. Low-salt diets, vitamin B$_6$ (300 mg per day), and diuretics have been used with some success. (O,F)

Diarrhea: Frequent unformed stools, sometimes accompanied by stomach pain or cramping. Could be caused by food sensitivity, too many raw vegetables (especially lettuce), lactose intolerance, or intestinal protein overload seen with Optifast or other high-protein diets. There should be no blood in stool! Check diet, eliminate possible causes, and give intestinal tract a rest with bland liquids for one day. (O,F)

Dizziness: Feeling of whirling—either the room is whirling around you or you are whirling. This is usually not a symptom that comes from dieting, although occasionally low blood sugar will precipitate it. Generally it is a sign of middle ear infection. Try some orange juice if it persists. (R,M,F)

Dry mouth: Usually a result of heavy fluid loss during a diet. Diet pills and diuretics can make it worse, but it can be present even without them. (C,M,F)

Dry skin: Skin gets dryer with age—it loses its water content, there is a decrease of sweat and sebaceous gland output, and the sun has been poisoning it more with each passing year. Weight-loss dieting can also cause dry skin and none of the mechanisms are the same. It could be a drop in the fat intake, but that seems unlikely the body is breaking down so much fat, even if it isn't being ingested. It can't be vitamins because we supplement them vigorously. A more likely explanation would be the drop in metabolic rate. So to correct for dry skin naturally, stimulate the thyroid gland with iodine or kelp. (O,F)

Gas bloating, abdominal pain *(flatus).* Your usual diet is altered in a weight-loss program, and now includes more of foods not ordinarily eaten such as the "aromatic vegetables"—cabbage, cauliflower, and broccoli—and more low-calorie products containing Sorbitol, the large undigestible sugar molecule found in sugarless gums and candies. You also tend to drink more low-calorie carbonated beverages. Watch diet and have some simethicone handy (an inert substance that absorbs gas). (C,M,F)

Hair loss (alopecia): Mild scalp hair loss often follows long-term (over two months) low-calorie dieting (under 850 calories daily). This problem reverses itself within several months after reintroduction of normal eating. However the hair that returns is sometimes not of the same quality and thickness. The new antibaldness drug Minoxydyl might be helpful here, assuming it's approved for general use. (A,F)

Headache: There are many causes for headaches on a diet because there are many different kinds of headaches. They range from the simple tension headache (relieved by a mild pain pill or muscle relaxant) to the throbbing vascular headache or migraine, brought about by changes in diet, allergies, or low potassium. Some of the more common diet headaches could be the result of a decreased plasma volume—better known as dehydration—that is often a part of early weight loss. It responds well to increased fluid intake. Diet-type headaches should not be accompanied by vomiting or any changes in eyesight (although migraine sufferers see spots). (C,F)

Hives (urticaria): Itchy pink bumps that appear and disappear on the body. They usually signal a food or drug allergy. Diuretics are a common cause. Initially, a mild antihistamine like Benadryl can be used with a topical corticoid ointment to stop the itching. Once they start popping out, however, more and more things can make them appear, until it seems you are allergic to everything. If the hives become larger and spread over most of the body, that could signal a real emergency state in which breathing becomes more difficult. Get to a hospital—adrenalin and steroids can be used to good effect. (C,M,F)

Insomnia: The inability to fall asleep, or, once asleep, to stay asleep. Can be caused by diet pills, ketosis, caffeine in coffee and diet soda, thyroid, and alcohol. Discontinue all stimulating agents. Try a glass of milk or some protein at bedtime. They are good sources of tryptophan, which raises brain serotonin, which in turn promotes sleep. (C,F)

Light-headedness: A feeling of being slightly off balance, "spacey," faint. Sometimes mistaken for dizziness. In the first part of a diet it can be due to the large water loss, which depletes blood volume and electrolytes and potassium in particular. This can cause a drop in blood pressure (hypotension), especially when changing from a sitting to standing position. It can also be due to a drop in blood sugar (hypoglycemia) brought about by reduced carbohydrates in the diet. (C,M,F)

Menstrual irregularities: Irregular periods can become regular with weight loss. Often cramps get worse, perhaps indicating ovulatory cycles are restored as body weight comes closer to normal. Going below set-point weight will make periods less frequent and scanty. No dietary change should make periods heavier, although occasionally this will happen. The rhythm method of birth control does not work well during weight-loss dieting, as the time of ovulation can change. (C,F)

Muscle cramps: Sometimes referred to as charley horses—painful spasms of calf, inner thigh, instep, or finger muscles. The most frequent cause is low potassium, although occasionally calcium supplements will help the symptoms. For immediate relief, extend the muscle in the opposite direction of the cramp, take potassium supplements, and apply heat to the area. (C,M,F)

Nausea: Sick, queasy feeling, often brought about by taking vitamins, especially the B vitamins, on an empty stomach. Sometimes, however, a low potassium level causes this. Since supplemental potassium can be a stomach irritant, this in itself can cause nausea. Watch pill intake and eat some easily digestible high-potassium foods like spinach broth with a piece of melba toast. (O,M,F)

Overstimulation: Feelings of hyperactivity, nervousness, increased energy, difficulty sleeping. Seen with the use of certain diet pills, or excessive coffee drinking and smoking. The metabolic state of ketosis is stimulating to males in particular. Stop or decrease stimulants, and buffer the nervous system with a mild analgesic like Tylenol. (O,M,F)

Palpitations: Skipped heartbeats, sometimes referred to as "butterflies in the chest." The heart momentarily loses its rhythm, skips a beat, and the next beat is stronger and noticeable. Palpitations are indications of heart muscle irritability and can be caused by caffeine, diet pills, exercise, fatigue, and low potassium. They can be frightening, but are usually benign. Eliminate the causal factor if you can identify it, and try to relax when you experience them. If they persist for any length of time, check with your doctor.

Shortness of breath: Breathlessness usually after exercise. This improves with dieting, but if it returns, it could mean low body potassium. Supplement with pills or food. (O,F)

Stomach pain: This could either be the gnawing pain of hunger, the sharp shooting pains of gas, the burning pain of inflammation of the stomach, or the spasms of an irritated bowel. Interval feedings of low-calorie foods should help the hunger pains. Simethicone should absorb the gas. Food sensitivity could be causing the irritated bowel, and this should happen relatively soon after the food has been ingested, so you can identify the offender and eliminate it. Burning pain is usually not part of normal stomach sensation and could be caused by ingesting aspirin or chocolate, drinking alcohol, or taking potassium supplements. Any pain that persists requires medical attention. Fever and vomiting are *not* associated with dieting. (O,M,F)

Weakness: A feeling of extreme fatigue, not related to normal activity, manifested by difficulty raising an arm or legs (to climb stairs), or even difficulty combing hair. This is usually the sign of a low potassium level, brought about by a successful diet where intake of high-potassium foods has not balanced loss or by the use of water pills (diuretics). Even with potassium-sparing diuretics (Dyazide and Modiuretic), you can still have significant drops in potassium if you're dieting. If you don't have a potassium supplement handy, drink four ounces of orange juice with a pinch of salt (just in case sodium levels are a little low). (C,M,F)

INDEX